Ps

CONFLICT BETWEEN ENERGY AND URBAN ENVIRONMENT

Consolidated Edison Versus the City of New York

Regina Axelrod
Adelphi University

UNIVERSITY
PRESS OF
AMERICA

Copyright © 1982 by
University Press of America, Inc."
P.O. Box 19101, Washington, D.C. 20036

ISBN (Perfect): 0-8191-2377-3
ISBN   (Cloth): 0-8191-2376-5

Library of Congress Number: 80-67179

To Gregg, Lenny and
all my students past and present, may
we continue to learn together, opening
each new book of knowledge with humility

TABLE OF CONTENTS

LIST OF TABLES..ix

PREFACE..xi

CHAPTER ONE

    INTRODUCTION...1

        The Energy Problem.................................2
            Problems of Electric Power Generation

        The Environmental Problem..........................9
            Perceptions of the Environmental Problem

        Conflict Among Competing Values....................15

        Description of Decision Situation..................18

        Con Edison Prior to 1970...........................24

        Characteristic of Decision Situations..............26

CHAPTER TWO

    DECISION-MAKING..36

        The Usefulness of Studying Decision-Making.........36

        Definition of a Decision...........................37

        The Rational-Comprehensive Model...................38
            Advantages of the Rational Model
            Limitations of the Rational Model

        The Incremental Model..............................41
            Advantages of the Incremental Model
            Limitations of the Incremental Model

        Rational-Incremental Decision-Making Dichotomy.....48

        Case Study Analysis................................53

CHAPTER THREE

THE SETTING...60

    The Environmental Protection Agency (EPA).......62

    The Federal Energy Office (FEO).................66

    The Army Corps of Engineers.....................68

    The New York State Department of Environmental
    Conservation (DEC)..............................69

    The Public Service Commission (PSC).............71

    The New York City Environmental Protection
    Administration (CEPA)...........................72

    The Mayor's Office..............................76

    Consolidated Edison (Con Edison)................78

    Conclusion......................................81

CHAPTER FOUR

PROPOSITIONS DERIVED FROM CASE STUDIES: PROPOSITIONS
1 THROUGH 7...86

    Proposition 1...................................86
        The Astoria Controversy
        The 1973 Fuel Crisis
        Summary

    Proposition 2..................................105
        The Astoria Controversy
        The 1973 Fuel Crisis

    Proposition 3..................................112
        The Astoria Controversy
        The 1973 Fuel Crisis
        Summary

    Proposition 4..................................116
        The Astoria Controversy
        The 1973 Fuel Crisis
        Summary

Proposition 5...................................125
    The Astoria Controversy
    The 1973 Fuel Crisis
    Summary

Proposition 6...................................140
    The Astoria Controversy
    The 1973 Fuel Crisis
    Summary

Proposition 7...................................154
    The Astoria Controversy
    The 1973 Fuel Crisis

Conclusion......................................160

CHAPTER FIVE

    CONCLUSION......................................176

BIBLIOGRAPHY..185

LIST OF TABLES

Table   Page

1-1   Federal Standards for Sulfur Dioxide.....20

1-2   Federal Standards for Particulates.......21

2-1   Imports of Residual Fuel Oil by Percent
         Sulfur Content to New York State.......163

PREFACE

This book is written with the hope that issues surrounding the environmental impact of energy policies shall soon be considered significant enough to the public and their representatives in government, that the ends of policymaking shall guide the decision-making process and not the reverse.

I would like to express my appreciation to colleagues and friends who inspired and assisted me in the preparation of this manuscript. AnnMarie Walsh, Institute of Public Administration, Marilyn Gittel, Graduate Center, City University of New York, Kenneth Sherill, Hunter College, Christa Altensetter, City University of New York, Dan Rustow, Graduate Center, City University of New York and Robert Engler, Graduate Center, City University of New York were most helpful in guiding me through the ongoing research. The suggestions of Charles O. Jones, University of Pittsburgh, Martin Landau, University of California at Berkeley, Lettie Wenner, University of Illinois and Walter Rosenbaum, University of Florida were helpful in the reorganization of the material. To those who were called upon to proofread the manuscript I am deeply grateful - Serena Axelrod, Rena Katz, Pat Belizaire, Bonnie Bluh and especially Leonard Kahn who watched the project mature and was always available for support and advice. For keeping all things together in addition to deciphering and typing, I am forever indebted to Deborah Heineman, Administrative Assistant, Institute for Suburban Studies, Adelphi University. I was also fortunate to have received the support and confidence of my colleagues in the Political Studies Department and Administration, Adelphi University.

CHAPTER 1

INTRODUCTION

This study is focused upon particular styles of decision-making, the forces that encourage some styles and discourage others, and the impact of decision styles on outcomes. The subject of decision-making in political science is a broad and variegated one that has been approached in different ways. Styles of decision-making or the characteristics of choice process are the central variables considered here. Other groups of variables--history, interest group configurations, leadership, distribution of political power--are viewed secondarily as they affect decision styles.

Other approaches which enhance the study of the same problems include the following: (1) study of the power configurations of various actors, comparing the relative strengths of elected officials, administrative personnel and private sector actors; (2) analysis of interest groups and constituencies and their support of specific values; (3) analysis of non-decision-making characteristics of issues whereby the agenda is controlled by structure, history and distribution of resources; (4) the role of the government as a regulatory force and protector of the public interest in conflict with demands from the regulated for greater protection, and bureaucratic vested interests. As regulatory agencies are increasingly concerned with satisfying their respective constituencies, broader public interests may be ignored.

The author does not pursue these alternative approaches as a major focus, although they are not neglected in as much as they contribute to an

understanding of decision-making styles. The
central focus here is an examination of the
conflict between environmental protection and
energy usage, more specifically, the political
management of environmental issues resulting
from electric power generation within the large
urban areas of metropolitan New York City. The
issue which confronts government is how to balance
public demand for power with the commitment to
protect the environment. Environment and energy
values are represented in the political arena by
public and private actors on three levels of
authority - local, state and national. The context
for examining this conflict is the decision-making
process itself. It is suggested that decision-
making (on a continuum from incremental to
rational-comprehensive) will affect not only the
resolution of the conflict, but the manner in
which it is placed on the public agenda.

Energy/environment politics are complex,
involving intense interrelationships with other
public issues. The characteristics of these
politics include: (1) heavy dependence on
specialized knowledge; (2) direct impact on
private economic interests; (3) technical need
for integrative decision-making; and (4) involvement of major values which affect the survival of
humankind. The author analyzes how government
officials have coped with these problems by
utilizing two case studies of political decision-
making in New York City in the early 1970's.

The Energy Problem

In a rapidly expanding industrial economy,
consumer demands for energy to support production
were met with little regard for environmental
consequences. Government policies that stimulated
private investment in the exploitation of natural
resources included land grants, oil depletion
allowances, and a "hands off" attitude toward the
extraction of coal and oil reserves.

In an energy-intensive society, energy
consumption increases at a slightly lower rate
than GNP. In the U.S., the average annual
percentage growth rates for GNP and energy consumption from 1950-1965 were 3.7% and 3% respectively.[1] Higher energy consumption can be
traced to greater amounts of energy required to
sustain a modern industrial economy and advanced
living standards.[2] Therefore, energy consumption
will increase at a faster rate than population.
Between 1960 and 1972, while annual per capita
oil consumption increased 3.5%, population growth
increased 2% per annum.[3]

Public attitudes toward energy have traditionally been based on fulfilling consumer demand
requirements at whatever level they were desired.
It was assumed that supplies would remain unlimited
and uninterrupted. Even the early conservation
movement did not deviate from this ideology.
Early twentieth century government conservation
policies have recently been criticized for being
less concerned with the scarcity of resources than
with the exploitation of raw materials for development.[4] "The first principle of conservation is
development," wrote the conservationists, "the
use of natural resources now existing on this
continent for the benefit of people who live here is
now."[5]

Between 1965-1975, energy consumption grew
more rapidly than domestic supplies of fuel and
nuclear energy. Because of historic public
expectation of unlimited supply, the contemporary
public is unprepared to deal with problems of
scarcity. Interruptions of energy supplies affect
almost every household. The effect is the same
if shortages are contrived by fuel producers in
order to increase prices. When gasoline supplies
fell in the early 1970's, every automobile owner
felt the impact of gasoline shortages. (An
earlier experience involving control of gasoline
supplies occurred during World War II, when the
Petroleum Administration for War directed the

3

Office of Price Administration to ration gasoline,
going so far as to ban all non-essential driving
in 1943.[6] The Arab embargo of supplies, especially to the northeastern United States during the
winter of 1973-1974, resulted in inflated prices.
As a result, the public became more aware of its
dependence on energy supplies. Interruption of
supplies had four major consequences: (1) it led
to stepped up research and development of alternate energy supplies; (2) it gave oil and coal
producers the opportunity to obtain approval for
projects previously rejected on environmental
grounds, e.g., the Alaska Pipeline; (3) it
encouraged demands for the deregulation of natural
gas, in order to give incentives to suppliers to
increase production by letting the price rise as
high as the market would allow; and (4) it resulted
in the relaxation of environmental restrictions by
allowing the use of high polluting fuels for
electric power generating plants and the proliferation of nuclear power plants. In summary,
interruption of energy supplies shifted political
balance back in favor of fuel producers, and
limited resources, rather than unlimited, became
the argument for maximum exploitation. The New
York Times reported that commercial interests
were having a field day: "...They are trying to
undo the progress of the past five years in the
name of an energy crisis that is being success-
fully misinterpreted and misserved by everyone
involved."[7]

It has been suggested by some authors that
the Arab embargo of oil was not the precipitating
factor in the increased price for oil or its
scarcity.[8] Between 1970 and 1973, United States
demand for foreign oil increased, due in part to
a decrease in domestic output while United States
energy consumption needs were increasing.[9] While
oil came to be the preferred fuel over coal by
electric utilities for environmental reasons
and demands for gasoline increased, the fact that
United States' oil companies were spending more

4

capital in foreign rather than domestic investment tightened domestic supplies.

The major oil companies were concerned that if the foreign producing countries demanded greater participation in oil company decision-making, prices might be affected. As they reduced sales of crude oil and tightened the market, forcing third party buyers into competition, these profits were not shared by the host countries. "As crude oil costs rose, the oil companies raised prices...to an extent greater than would have been justified by the rise in crude costs alone."[10] By September 1973, the oil producing nations demanded a share of the profits that the oil companies were getting on the market. (Between January 1, 1973 and October 16, 1973 the market price for oil increased from $2.27 to $3.54 per barrel.)[11] Prices were therefore increasing well before the Arab embargo and supplies were curtailed.

The embargo on Middle Eastern oil was not successful as oil continued to flow from non-embargo countries, e.g., Iran and Nigeria; unreported oil stored in tankers continued to their destination; and increased imports of Arab oil in the early part of 1973 eased the supply situation.

Problems of Electric Power Generation

The production of electricity involves the transfer of one form of energy into another. In steam generating units, the combustion of oil or coal releases heat. This heat changes water into steam, which expands through a turbine, producing electricity. The steam is then condensed to water and either returned to the boiler or discarded. In fossil fuel plants, 60-70% of the heat produced by the combustion process is returned to the environment as waste heat, since such energy cannot be stored. Thus, because of the inefficiency of the combustion process, most heat produced by fossil fuel electric generating plants produces

5

unintended side-effects by artificially warming
both the atmosphere and adjacent bodies of water.
Moreover, between 8% and 9% of electricity generated may be lost during transmission.

Electric utility plants are a major user of
fossil fuels. In 1968, 50% of American utilities
used coal and 7% used oil to fire their generators.[12]
Electric power generation also used up ½ of the
United States coal production in 1967 and more than
¾ of the total annual residual oil supply in 1968.[13,14]
The production of electricity has increased over the
last 40 years, while its price - relative to other
goods and services - has declined. From 1928 to
1968, electric rates declined from an average of
2.71 cents per kilowatt (KW) to 1.55 cents per KW,
while the Consumer Price Index doubled. During this
period of time, per capita electric consumption
increased eightfold while the total revenues received
by utilities increased ninefold.[15] The public assumed
that continued growth of electric utilities would
result in a continued drop in unit cost for consumers.[16]

Dependence on electric power grew as industry
and utilities together undertook promotional activities.
Electrical appliances, high-rise construction with
total temperature regulation, and all-electric private
homes became commonplace. Advertising campaigns
stimulated public desire for increased electric
power.[17] To meet this growing demand, utilities
constructed more and larger facilities, and to fully
utilize these new facilities, promotional activities
were intensified to ensure greater demand. Again,
more demand produced still newer facilities, and so
the cycle continued.

The Federal Power Commission (FPC) forecasted
in 1969 that electric power requirements (i.e. demands)
during the period 1970-1990 would increase fourfold
in the Northeast.[18] This is probably a conservative
estimate, since the projection for electric power
demand made in 1952 for 1,400 billion KW hours in
1975 were surpassed as early as 1968.[19] It was
projected in 1969 that the historical annual 7%
growth rate for electric consumption, doubling energy

volume in under a decade, would continue until the 1990's.[20] To meet this demand, utilities would have to build 900 million KW of new capacity by 1990, as well as find 225 sites for facilities of 500 megawatts (MW) or larger.[21] However, trends up until 1980 indicate that the growth rate for electricity has leveled off. Utilities explain that it is their "mission" to meet demand: "...As long as general growth is sought or permitted, the growth in the use of electric power is both necessary and constructive."[22] Indeed, Consolidated Edison of New York (Con Ed), as a public utility, is obligated by New York State law to supply electric power to its 8,650,000 customers.

Utilities contend that new energy demands should be met because reliable availability of electric power has a positive effect on living standards. Cheap electricity provides lower income groups with an opportunity to enjoy appliances and other amenities that make life more comfortable. The utilities also argue that electric power is a clean form of energy that actually produces environmental benefits; mass transit facilities powered by electricity are environmentally preferable to expanded automobile travel. Dependence upon electric power for numerous essential services (i.e., subways, ventilation, and lighting) has been a crucial component in the growth of our cities. One need only to recall the blackout of 1965 in New York City to understand just how closely our lives are tied to electric power. Utilities also maintain that building new facilities has a secondary effect on living standards by providing construction and maintenance employment (a factor that usually engenders labor support for utility projects).

In order to fulfill the mandate of providing electricity, utilities must contend with external constraints. Utilities are faced with high interest rates on borrowing; high costs due to requirements to conform to air and water quality regulations; increases in fuel prices; frequent equipment failure and construction delays; and prolonged governmental approval procedures. Higher costs are particularly burdensome since 50% of a utilities'

costs are fixed and unrelated to output. Most of a
utility's assets are fixed in plant and equipment.
The economics of scale achieved in the 1960's were
offset by inflation and technological limits.
Recently, the costs incurred by utilities have
increased faster than the national inflation rate.

A major source of capital for utilities is
bonds. The interest charged is related to market
conditions and the bond rating from major bond
rating agencies. When bond ratings decline, the
increased change in interest rate can be substantial.
Moreover, in New York State, a BB rating can make
those bonds ineligible as a legal investment for
financial institutions. (Between February and June
1974, 14 utilities had their ratings downgraded
which resulted in increased debt cost and affected
the marketability of the bonds.)[23]

Increased costs due to inflation and debt
charges affect construction. In 1964, new generating facilities cost between $100 and $150 per KW.
In 1974 the cost was estimated at $500.

Moreover, since rate increases have not kept
pace with higher costs, earnings have been eroded
and construction of new facilities have been post-
poned. Fifty-two companies reported their 1974-1978
construction budgets were reduced by $8.3 billion.
This represented about 65 plants.[24]

Efforts by utilities to urge their customers
to conserve electricity have hurt some utilities.
Since major utility costs are fixed, declining
revenues due to successful conservation efforts have
left utilities with increased financial burdens
which may be transferred to the customer in the form
of higher rates.

Utilities were hit by higher prices for residual
oil even before the Arab embargo of October 1973,
while the prices for other refined products increased
at a lower rate, i.e. while gasoline prices increased
95.4%, residual oil increased 224.2% from 1972 to 1974.[25]
One explanation is that the easier it is to pass costs

on to customers, the higher the price will be. Private utilities may pass higher fuel costs on by increasing rates or with fuel riders added to bills.

Utilities have resisted air and water quality regulations because of their financial burdens. "There are those zealous ecologists who would cut down the demand rather than boost the supply, and if that makes the lights go out eventually, well at least we will have our beautiful unspoiled environment."[26] Regulations which restrict the use of "dirty" high-sulfur oil, which is cheaper than low-sulfur oil, do add to the consumer's bill. Recent court challenges to the construction of new facilities because of their environmental impact have caused costly delays. According to a 1970 FPC National Power Survey, one fourth of new plants were behind construction schedule, and 39% of these delays were due to environmental and regulatory problems.[27] Such setbacks tend to increase the total cost of construction in a period of inflation. Locating new facilities outside metropolitan areas also increases construction costs because of the greater expense of transmission and distribution. According to Joseph Swidler, a former TVA advisor, FPC Chairman and New York State Public Service Commission (PSC) Chairman, "Environmental requirements can contribute substantially to the cost of living and intensify inflationary pressures."[28]

The Environmental Problem

Certain features of environmental issues differentiate them from other policy areas. The environmental perspective is long-range. Not only do present actions produce effects which will be felt far into the future, but solutions to environmental problems require an extended time frame for observable results.

Discrete actions in environmental policy have a cumulative effect. Although individual decisions may appear rational, ecologist Garrett Hardin points

out that, when numerous decisions are considered
collectively, they accrue unanticipated consequences.[29]
For example, Austin Heller and Edward Ferrand point
out that pollutants interacting with each other may
have a more damaging effect than if present independ-
ently in the atmosphere.[30] Similarly, project-by-
project evaluation of local actions often overlook
the aggregate effect on the environment.

Secondary or unintended consequences of discrete
actions are often due to the exclusion of social costs
from the market system. For instance, a decision to
dump wastes from a cement plant into a river as part
of an economically efficient production process may
not only pollute the river, but affect marine and
plant life for decades to come. The social costs are
simply not reflected in the producer's price and therefore the decision is socially inefficient.[31] Again,
an individual cannot purchase an amount of clean air.
Air may be a free good, but clean air is not.[32] The
consequences of both the common ownership of resources
and the absence of pricing mechanisms to safeguard
them has been the overuse and pollution of these
resources.[33]

Another characteristic of environmental issues
is their interdependency. Failure to perceive interactive processes in the environment, or disregard
of their interrelated totality, is due in part to
lack of knowledge about these processes and to the
segmental nature with which policy problems are
customarily handled. Environmental policies have
effects which spill over into other policy areas
such as economic growth, banking, and real estate.
The resulting problems are complex because they
usually follow from a number of separate, discrete
decisions, and therefore have multiple origins.

Evaluating potential uses of resources held in
common is extremely complex because the optimal level
for each use depends on the individual's own evaluation.
"To one it is estuaries to nourish ducks for hunters
to shoot, to another it is factory land."[34] Comparison

10

of these goods with each other is impossible because
they are incommensurable, and incommensurables cannot
be weighted in common units of measurement.

A final feature of environmental issues that
differentiate them from other policy areas is its
inadequate representation by organized constituencies.
The bargaining among competitive interest groups and
politicians - bargaining that is characteristic of
the American political system - discounts environmental
goals. The environmental constituency is broadly
based and heterogeneous, becoming effective only in
periodic "revivals" that generate acute but sporadic
public interest. Political leaders have difficulty
calculating how to exchange support of environmental
policies for support at the polls. Moreover, politicians tend to be wary of tackling environmental
issues because such challenges to "the system" are
too complex for them to handle by traditional methods.[35]
Finally, environmental groups, hard pressed for
financial backing, tend to be weak lobbies. Referring
to such public interest groups, Grant McConnell notes,
"Their absence from or, at best, their ineffective
presence upon the political scene leaves a largely
open field for the success of those more concrete and
narrow interests whose mutual opposition is not
great."[36]

Perceptions of the Environmental Problem

Proposals for coping with environmental problems
reflect attitudes about causes of the environmental
condition. Some perceive environmental problems as
incidental to the normal functioning of the political
system and subject to corrective mechanisms (i.e.,
clean-up campaigns, construction of sewage systems,
or conservation of resources). Adherents of this
approach do not essentially challenge societal
patterns. Gerald Garvey, for example, suggests
technological modifications to improve the environment which include recycling, the use of nonpolluting
fuels, and efficient energy conservation processes.[37]

11

Other writers stress inadequate public planning and administrative action as fundamental to persistent environmental problems. Institutional response to environmental conditions through new laws and regulations has had less impact than anticipated because of weak planning and weak agencies. This perspective implies a need for greater governmental effort to balance interests more fairly. Cynthia Enloe suggests that the impetus for change be sought through more effective institutional mechanisms in the administration of environmental regulations.[38] Yet, the effectiveness of environmental agencies is a product of the subsystem of clientele and outside support, agency visibility, and level of resources, as well as the legitimacy of the agency in a complex bureaucratic setting. The problem of enforcing environmental agency regulations is also a function of agency resources. Esther Rodetti Schacter noted that competition among agencies for new funds inhibit an agency from fulfilling program goals.[39] The lack of commitment of power and resources can be attributed partially to weak public support.[40] To overcome this problem, McClellan suggests that new regional agencies be established with the support of public groups to counter strong industry pressures on local governments. Such agencies should have broad powers to impose fines and to issue subpoenas and permits.[41]

Environmental problems may also be analyzed in terms of market economics. Regulation through taxation and monetary incentives is considered adequate by some writers as a means to force polluters to be responsible for the environmental costs they generate.[42]

Critics of those relying on market incentives, however, argue that such policies may drive small companies out of business while larger enterprises which can afford the fines, will gladly "pay to pollute". Moreover, since air is not an unlimited good, as James C. Hite reasons, the price of air in a theoretical market model would reflect the cost of pollution.[43] However, since an individual cannot bargain for clean air, new rules of allocation should

12

be created so that the price equitably reflects competition among users.

There is an additional objection to a market approach which utilizes supply and demand curves for environmental goods. Attempts have been made to find an optimal level of environmental quality using a cost-benefit approach - that is, by calculating the exchange of a unit of benefit for a unit of cost until the cost exceeds the benefit. Using the principle of marginalism, borrowed from classical economics, stress is placed on maximizing benefit until additional expansion begins to cost more than it is worth.[44] However, attempts to quantify such costs and benefits have been less than satisfactory. Barry Commoner argues that the cost of a particular economic process includes the environmental impact, which is an approximate measure of the degradation of environmental quality.[45] But, a method of calculating the worth of excess human deaths, loss of future earnings due to illness, and the inconvenience of chronic respiratory disease or aesthetic and psychic loss has yet to be developed. Such social costs or externalities are often omitted in cost-benefit analysis, even though they are inevitably by-products of an economic theory that treats the environment as a free good. Larry Ruff suggests that sometimes an economically inefficient policy may be desirable on distributional grounds despite its cost.[46] Unfortunately, if policy generates a net gain on a cost-benefit scale, that analysis does not provide for specifying who sustains the gains or losses - or what level of emotional intensity the losers might experience.[47] Moreover, relying on market analysis, forces manipulation of data and modes of analysis which fail to recognize the essence of the particular environmental problem. It narrows the range of alternatives and substitutes comprehensive analysis for meaningless and short-sighted forced calculations.

A comprehensive approach to environmental policy perceives problems as systemic. Since their origin is built into technological processes

13

and the economic system itself, solving them can
only result from a shift in the priorities and values
of the society. Not only are specific measures to
be taken by government, but a reformulation of the
government's role in environmental affairs is considered part of the long-range objectives of the
systemic approach.

Adherents of a comprehensive approach tend to
stress different aspects of the systemic solution.
Michael Kraft suggests that the level of change is
related to the system's acceptance of change and
reception to innovativeness.[48] The system must
consistently encourage criticism and participation
if new goals are to be sought. Lester Milbraith
emphasizes that social change will only "occur if
there are basic changes in values in our laws, and
in the structure or rewards in society."[49] Government alone, he maintains, has the resources to deal
with planned change. It is further argued that the
governmental role include public participation in
value formation based on human need by creating a
political structure to consider value judgments in
which the issue of adequate environmental quality
can be reformulated.[50] This would provide an
institutional means for influencing environmental
choices. (The mere creation of a new agency would
not automatically bring about such a change, without
a corresponding change in the perception of the roots
of environmental problems.) "It overlooks the
essential qualitative distinctions between a particular interest that is part of the productive dimen-
sion of society, and a problem-area of a communal
nature that concerns the relationship between the
industrial system itself and the overall environment
of life."[51] Such analysis must come to terms with
the traditional concepts of economic growth, profit,
and the notion of progress.

Lehtey and Edmunds suggest a new definition of
progress in terms of humanity's relation to the
environment. Rampant economic growth, unrestrained
technology and failure to appreciate the long-range

14

consequences of modern industrial production are
the real sources of system inequities.[52] Emphasizing
these dysfunctions, Robert Paul Wolff contends that
a system of private capitalism, no matter how benevolent and reform-oriented, may just be unable to
effect any change. Society may require a transforma-
tion, "...into objects of decision of important
matters which are now the consequence of uncoordinated
acts, rather than merely an alteration in the way in
which present power is employed."[53]

    The analysis of the environmental situation on
this more comprehensive level has also been emphasized
in the prolific work of Lynton Caldwell.[54] He
suggests an interdisciplinary approach utilizing
information from related fields to increase the
breadth and understanding of environmental problems.
This approach treats the environment as a totality
directing attention to the complexity and inter-
relatedness of interactive processes. Recognizing
that environmental problems usually involve a conflict
among public values, it is argued that the acquisition
of knowledge will make the choices clearer.

Conflict Among Competing Values

    The process of generating electricity has an
environmental impact. Due to increased public awareness of the effects of pollution, the government has
been called upon to take an active role in resolving
the conflict of providing adequate electric power
while minimizing the environmental impact. Government has also been forced into the arena when the
fossil fuels used to generate electricity have come
into short supply.

    Ironically, the very price competitiveness of
fuel-burning utilities - most welcome to consumers
of other industrial goods -.has been the concern of
environmental interest groups. When electric rates
remain stable or decline because of price competitive-
ness, the demand for electricity increases. To meet
new demand requires the construction of new fossil
fuel plants as well as rapid increase in the number

of nuclear power facilities. Not only would air and
water pollution increase, but the unknown hazards
of radiation from nuclear plants present an even
more ominous threat. The argument against slowing
the growth of utilities is based upon its effect
on the consumption of goods and services and unemployment. (It is now believed, that unemployment
is not directly related to utility output and that
employment could even increase with the development
of energy conservation industries.[55]) "The conflicts
between the consumption patterns that we all want
and the environmental ill-effects that we wish to
avoid is sharper for energy than for perhaps any
other aspect of natural resource use...everyone wants
to use as much electricity as he needs...yet few love
a power plant or transmission line."[56]

The nature of the conflicts is murky to the public.
Although the passage of the 1970 Clean Air Act seemed
a victory for environmentalists, President Nixon
undermined its effectiveness when he proposed measures
which would take the corporate costs of pollution
control into consideration in setting standards,
would eliminate the nondeterioration section of the
Act which protected nonpolluted areas, and would
allow suspension of environmental regulations, such
as pending automobile emission-standards. Nixon
also advocated a speed-up of nuclear power plant
licensing in spite of growing concern about safety
hazards.[57] The New York Times warned that "under the
pious guise or disguise of energy conservation, air
and water pollution standards are being dangerously
revised."[58] The Environmental Protection Agency
(EPA) emerged in the curious position of being undermined by the very President who had created it.
(The Ford and Carter administrations also did little
to support the EPA mission.) At bay from critics
contending that the energy crisis was partially
the result of environmentalists' efforts, the EPA
retorted, "The current energy crisis is now being
cited by those who fear the future as proof that
concern for the environment has already begun to
ruin us. They imply that we must abandon all this
environmental nonsense and use fuel anyway we please."[59]

16

Industry, business, real estate developers, and other special interest lobbies, can in this way, isolate the environmentalists from broader public support. As the battle for public opinion gained momentum, the general public became increasingly bewildered. No clear concept of the public interest emerged from opinion surveys, although the public has consistently believed that the environment was a problem.

The conflict between energy and environmental values may clearly be conceived as a conflict between very long-term public values and shorter term, more specific objectives. The clash emerges when diffuse long-term environmental concerns interfere with the satisfaction of immediate and pressing energy needs. Decision-makers tend to maximize the short-run because they are subject to the daily demands of their office. (Short-term goals may include meeting employment, expansion, land developers' requests, and consumers' electric power needs). "Responding to their most immediate and proximate stimuli, decision-makers behave so as to achieve and retain job security, standing and advancement, and to keep themselves and their organization out of political, economic, or other sorts of trouble...there is seldom any payoff for deciding in favor of, and committing resources to, such long-run and comprehensive goals as joining in a group effort to rid an entire metropolitan area of air and water pollution."[60] Where there is a conflict of values, it is pragmatic to sacrifice environmental values to ameliorate a crisis situation. Energy planning may require as much as a decade from proposal to production. Environmental impacts exceed a generation. Both, of course, involve time dimensions that far exceed the platform - election-record making cycle of politicians. But short-term power crises (due to shortages or dramatic price changes, threat-ened or actual) foreshorten power demands to a scale at which politicians facing elections must respond. The immediacy of a crisis (i.e., insufficient elec-tric power due to low system capacity during peak periods and/or fuel supplies) attracts immediate attention, forcing a choice between two values with

17

apparently incomparable time discounts. The lack of definition of the public interest - and how it can best be served - perpetuates the conflict by forcing decision-makers to try anew to balance these same interests every time a new crisis occurs, to reinvent the wheel. The characteristics of the conflict between energy and environment, therefore, should help test the hypothesis of this study; that the structure and styles of decision-making influence outcome; and that shifts in the structure and styles of decision-making are necessary conditions for changing the predominant patterns of policy that emerge from political processes.

Description of Decision Situation

This study focuses on the conflict in New York City - between potential health hazards and power shortages. Two cases were investigated. The first concerns Con Edison's action to obtain city approval for the construction of two new generating facilities. The second involves Con Edison's attempt to obtain a variance to the city's Air Code in order to allow the burning of high-sulfur fuel.

The time span of the field work on the cases from 1970 to 1974, provides enough perspective to observe continuity and development of patterns of decisional behavior among the actors. It was also a period when environmental issues gained prominence in the public arena and public criticism was being directed increasingly toward Con Edison.

The data collected from interviews of approximately 100 government, private sector and media respondents were compared with each other and with documentary and media sources in order to assess reliability and accuracy. Internal documents and correspondence files of Con Edison, city, state and federal agencies were studied. Administrative codes, statutes, and rulings were also examined. These primary sources were supplemented with secondary source material including books, periodicals, newspapers and journals.

18

The impact of power generation upon air quality can be profound because of sulfur dioxide and particulate emissions. In 1972, power plants in the United States emitted over 17 million tons of sulfur dioxide, or nearly 60% of all sulfur dioxides emitted into the atmosphere.[61] In New York City, the figure was less but still dramatic. In 1974, Con Edison's contribution to total sulfur dioxide emissions was 42.1%.[62]

It was the hazards of increased air pollution from Con Edison actions which brought opposition from the environmentalists, projecting the issue into the public purview. One of the major pollutants of sulfur fuel combustion is sulfur dioxide. The combination of sulfur dioxide and particulates (which are produced during the combustion process because of either incomplete combustion or vaporized materials which later condense) have been found to cause demonstratable health effects: the young, old, and chronically ill are especially vulnerable during periods of high sulfur and particulate exposure. Particulates which enter the respiratory tract in the presence of sulfur dioxide are particularly dangerous because the subsequent production of sulfuric acid can result in tissue damage. Even short-term exposures have been linked to cancer, bronchitis, emphysema, tuberculosis, and heart disease. One study estimates that nationally 110,000 deaths per year can be attributed to air pollution.[63] In New York City alone, there are an estimated 1,000-2,000 such deaths per year.[64] Significantly, the death rate for cancer of the respiratory tract is twice as high in urban areas where power plants are concentrated, than it is in rural areas.[65] In New York City from 1963-1968, 12% of the total daily mortality was related to air pollution.[66] The years 1969-1972 saw only a slight reduction from previous years.

Although the amount of sulfur dioxide emissions from Con Edison plants is substantial, the impact of this figure is somewhat diluted because of dispersion of the pollutants from Con Edison's high elevated smokestacks. In 1970, most areas of New

19

York City surpassed minimum federal and state standards for sulfur dioxide and particulate emissions by as much as three times.

TABLE 1-1

Federal Standards and Levels for Sulfur Dioxide

	Sulfur Dioxide City-wide					Federal Standards
	1969	1970	1971	1972	1973	
Arithmetic Mean	.80	.77	.40	.24	.26	.3 ppm annual aver.[a]
Times Exceeded .14	b	-	23	4	13	.14 ppm 24 hr. concentration to be exceeded once per year
Highest Daily Average	.49	.31	.22	.18	.36	

a
 parts per million
b
 not available

Source: Environmental Protection Administration

20

TABLE 1-2

Federal Standards and Levels for Particulates

	Particulates City-wide				Federal Standards
Geometric Average	98	104	105	82	75 ug/m^3 [a]
Daily Peak	608	581	579	256	260 ug/m^3

[a]micrograms per cubic meter

Source: Environmental Protection Administration

Certain areas of the city (especially around the East River) are more severly affected by Con Edison emissions than are other areas where standards are being met. The latter condition is primarily due to the mandatory switch to low-sulfur fuel in power generation and space heating. The city was naturally anxious to preserve these gains; this entailed both the maintenance of environmental restrictions and prevention of the development of new stationary sources of pollution.

Con Edison's case for building additional sources of power and using higher-polluting fuels was based on the threat of power shortages. In 1970, although Con Edison claimed that new installed capacity was needed to meet consumer electric demand, the city's newly formed environmental agency (CEPA) argued that (1) Con Edison had not explored alternatives to meet its projected power shortage of 1974, and that (2) the impact on air quality would be so severe as to

result in a health hazard. CEPA did not challenge
Con Edison's estimate of future peak load needs, but
argued there were other ways of meeting those needs.

The City Environmental Protection Administration
(CEPA) claimed that Con Edison overestimated its
reserve requirements in order to justify acquiring
greater installed capacity. The FPC requirement was
between 20-25%; according to CEPA, without new construction in Astoria there would still be a reserve
capacity of 27.7%. This figure omitted outside
purchases of electric power which would have augmented
reserve capacity. From 1970-1973, Con Edison had
purchased power from outside sources, and there was
no reason to believe this practice would change.

Con Edison also projected a 36.2% reserve capacity
for 1974, justifying that figure by emphasizing possible
delay of other plants under construction. However,
Con Edison included an 800 MW Astoria unit in its
figures of planned reserves for 1974 which inflated
the reserve figure. CEPA noted, "...The Company cannot
justify the Astoria expansion by claiming that it has
inadequate reserves in 1974 owing to possible construction delays and at the same time include Astoria as one
of the machines which might be delayed."[67]

CEPA concluded that the Astoria project, although
referred to by Con Edison as a base-load plant (i.e.,
designed to run efficiently at high loads) was really
being sought by Con Edison to meet its inflated peaking
demands. Peak projections are used to justify capacity
requirements and are an important part of appeals for
rate increases before the PSC.

CEPA also took issue with Con Edison's estimate
of the impact upon air quality by the construction of
a new plant. While Con Edison claimed that environmental deterioration caused by the Astoria plant would
be negligible, CEPA estimated that it would contribute
.15 ppm to the 24-hour average, which was already well
above standards.[68] CEPA estimated that if Astoria
used a .37% sulfur fuel, it would emit 15,000 tons per
year of sulfur oxides - 10% of total sulfur oxide
emissions for the entire city in 1975. This represented

between .02-.03 ppm of the total annual average.
When combined with other sources, levels would reach
.04-.06 ppm (annual average), ruling out any possibility of meeting the federal primary standards of
.03 ppm. [69]

Con Edison's proposal for the expansion of one
of its generating plants might have been handled more
privately had the environment not become a salient
issue and had not the newly formed CEPA been eager to
establish itself as a legitimate power in the city.
Con Edison provided city environmentalists and
politicians an opportunity to do battle. In 1970,
Mayor John Lindsay, anticipating a presidential
campaign, saw no immediate harm in letting CEPA pursue
its goal. Likewise, in 1973 his "lame duck" administration did not have to worry about political repercussions if the city refused to allow Con Edison to
burn high-polluting fuel.

Con Edison had traditionally resisted the im-
position of city regulations regarding low-sulfur
fuel. 60% of Con Edison's oil originates from the
Middle East or North Africa. (The sulfur content of
oil from other sources is usually too high to meet
regulations, i.e., Venezuela.) In response to the
fuel shortage of 1973, Con Edison expressed the fear
that, if their supply of low-sulfur fuel were not
replenished, there could be a power shortage. Again,
the city and Con Edison disagreed over severity of the
fuel shortage, the availability of low-sulfur fuel
from suppliers, and the effect of using higher-sulfur
fuel upon air quality. CEPA's primary concern was the
protection of gains made in air quality during preceed-
ing years. "The amount of sulfur oxides emitted is
directly proportional to the amount of fuel burned
and the sulfur content of the fuel."[70] CEPA policy
crystallized: limit the amount of high-sulfur fuels
burned in the city.

Both issues initiated by Con Edison were placed
on the public agenda in what appeared to be a crisis
atmosphere. The issues clearly brought into conflict
the short-run goal of meeting electric power needs and

23

the long-term goal of maintaining and improving air
quality standards. Compounding the difficulties
normally incurred in crisis decision-making, the
very data provided by Con Edison and by CEPA differed -
when it existed at all.

Con Edison Prior to 1970

New York City is completely dependent upon Con
Edison to provide electric power to an area populated
by 9 million inhabitants. Its 2.8 million customers
are mainly residential and commercial users with a
lower than national average per capita consumption
of electricity[71] (due to a low level demand in the
industrial sector and preponderance of apartment
dwellings.) Con Edison has the largest amount of
assets of any privately owned utility in the United
States, with approximately 250,000 stockholders.

Nevertheless, Con Edison suffers from a rather
low public image. Con Edison was the object of hostil-
ity by the Queens community in 1962 when it attempted
to obtain a license from the Atomic Energy Commission
(AEC) for a nuclear powered plant at Ravenswood,
Queens. The alleged lack of safety precautions for
a densely populated area generated such intense
opposition that the plan was abandoned.

Con Edison is caught between balancing the
interests of the stockholder, customer and the community. The rates it charged prior to 1970 were the
highest in the nation; Con Edison attributed this to
incurred high fuel costs, labor and interest charges,
a cash-flow problem, and a high tax bill. (Until
September 1973, the greater electricity use, the less
per kilowatt was charged.)[72]

Con Edison has additional problems: (1) Maintenance costs on its transmission system are high because
most of its cables are underground. (2) Con Edison
estimates that its major cost items are taxes and
fuel. In 1975, fuel accounted for 33¢ and taxes for
24¢ of every dollar billed to the customer. (3) Con
Edison costs for fuel and purchased power have increased

24

appreciably from $397.6 million in 1972 to $969.9
million in 1976. (The larger portion of this increase
was due to the rise in oil prices.) (4) Accounts
receivables owed to Con Edison amounted to $302,203,000
in 1975 down from $320,979,000 in 1974. This still
was a substantial amount of outstanding funds. (5) Con
Edison is required by the PSC to keep a 45 day reserve
for residual oil, which is expensive. (6) In the past,
Con Edison had overestimated its reserve capacity to
compensate for equipment failure. Old equipment had
been given unrealistically high capacity ratings and
the result was summer brown-outs due to breakdowns.
The severe 1965 blackout, coupled with generally poor
servicing, damaged Con Edison's reputation and strengthened its tendency to maximize generation capacity
(rather than to minimize power loss and encourage
conservation, for example.) The utility became the
object of criticism by the media, the press, and
political leaders.

Con Edison's financial problems surfaced when it
failed to pay a quarterly dividend to its stockholders
for the first time in the company's history in April
1974. Con Edison had traditionally provided reliable
dividends for its investors. However, in the early
1970's severe financial problems shook this confidence.
In 1972, the PSC forced Con Edison to switch from pre-
financing to arrearage financing. This meant that Con
Edison now had to finance construction with bank loans
and then sell bonds to retire the bank debt rather than
selling the bonds first to finance construction. Con
Edison was able only to float two of the three bond
issues it had planned for 1973. Con Edison's immediate
problem was to obtain financing to cover the year's
operations. Although discussions about the sale of
two plants to the Power Authority of the State of
New York (PASNY) were underway, passage of the necessary legislation was not definite because some
legislators doubted that Con Edison's interpretation
of its financial situation was accurate, while others
were demanding that the monies received by the sale
be used to ease customer bills. The Company believed
that a new stock offering would be unsuccessful leaving
them the alternative of cancelling the first quarterly

25

dividend on April 23, 1974. This saved Con Edison
$27.7 million which the company claimed would ease
the cash-flow situation (due to lower earnings, failure to recover costs due to fuel price increases and
higher taxes.)

The effect in the financial world was immediate.
Con Edison's bond rating by Standard and Poor's fell
to BB. Other utilities' stocks were downgraded.
However, the bill authorizing the sale of two Con
Edison plants passed the state legislature on May 16,
1974. It provided that any loss in revenue due to a
transfer in customers to PASNY would be charged to
Con Edison's remaining customers.

Con Edison recovered sufficiently to pay its
second quarterly dividend. The company claimed that
conditions had improved as a result of increased
sales, the stabilization of oil prices and a temporary
rate increase. Since then, dividends have remained
stable increasing from $.85 in 1974, $1.20 in 1975 to
$1.60 in 1976.

Although there have been changes in management
and public relations campaigns have been mounted,
the company's image has not substantially improved.
Con Edison's increasing difficulties in its relations
with the city, its investors, and its customers provided the external situation in the two case studies
under consideration.

Characteristics of the Decision Situations

Both decision situations, considered here, share
common characteristics which influenced strategy,
procedure and outcome. These characteristics can be
summarized as follows:

(1) The lack of information available to decision-
makers limits resources used to formulate the decision.
In both cases, Con Edison retained a monopoly of information with respect to electric power capacity and fuel
supply. Other information, including the availability
of fuel and the effects of conservation techniques,

26

were unavailable to government participants at the
time a decision was required.

(2) The time frame of the decision situation had
a specific importance. One decision involved construction of a generating plant, and pressure was felt to
provide sufficient lead time for the plant to be completed before a projected shortage developed. The
second decision, whether to allow higher-polluting
fuel, required time lag to ensure that supplies of
conforming fuel would be available. Lack of options
because of the immediacy of the situation was a significant factor in both decisional processes.

(3) Each decision situation required action and
involvement by numerous decision-makers from various
agencies within different government hierarchies.
The environmental agencies, younger and less experienced,
faced older established power regulatory bureaucracies
as well as Con Edison in a clash of style as well as
of substantive issue. The new environmental agencies
found themselves spurring the older power regulatory
agencies on to a more aggressive stance with respect
to Con Edison.

While Con Edison has a monopolistic position in
providing electricity, the authority of governmental
agencies which have regulatory functions is fragmented.
National multiple government responsibility includes
the Army Corps of Engineers, the Environmental Protection
Agency, the Department of Energy, the Federal Energy
Regulatory Commission, the Federal Power Commission and
the Nuclear Regulatory Commission. New facilities
must be approved by the Public Service Commission, the
New York Board on Siting, the Electric Generation and the
Environment, and the Department of Environmental Conservation on the state level and numerous local agencies,
i.e., for building and boiler installation permits. These
cross-cutting responsibilities make coordination of
electric policy difficult for the government and cause
lengthy delays for Con Edison. Innumerable decision-
making conflicts among these agenices results in
procedural delays and lack of coordination. Furthermore, this dispersion of power as opposed to the
concentration of corporate power may tend to strengthen

27

the goals of the latter to the detriment of the public
interest.

(4) <u>All participants tried to project an image
that responsible action was being taken, and used the
media and press to obtain public sympathy and support.</u>
On the governmental side, symbolic action took precedence
over concrete action. Since decisions had to be made
quickly, statements, agreements, and promises were
made that primarily constituted good public relations,
not necessarily good decision-making.

Both situations were the result of initiatives
taken by Con Edison to which the city had to respond.
In both situations, influential power holders had a
great opportunity to exercise their will in matters
of governmental regulation without an opportunity for
mutual checking power to occur. During the period
between the two crisis situations, the major issues
were overlooked. Con Edison was no more accountable to
the city for its operations and actions in 1974 than
it had been in 1970.

CHAPTER 1

FOOTNOTES

1. Joel Darmstadter, Energy in the World Economy,
    (Baltimore: J. Hopkins, 1971), p. 37.

2. Ibid., p. 32.

3. Joel Darmstadter and Hans Landsberg, "The
    Economic Background" in Raymond Vernon (Editor),
    The Oil Crisis, (New York: W.W. Norton, 1976),
    p. 16.

4. Samuel P. Hays, "The Mythology of Conservation,"
    in Henry Jarret (Editor), Perspectives on Conser-
    vation, (Baltimore: J. Hopkins Press, 1958),
    p. 40.

5. Gifford Pinchot, "Conservation and Progressive
    Ideology," Donald Worster (Editor), American
    Environmentalism, 1860-1915, (New York: John
    Wiley, 1973), p. 83.

6. Harvey Mansfield, A Short Story of OPA, Office of
    Temporary Controls, GPO, Washington, 1947, p. 177.

7. New York Times, April 7, 1974, Editorial.

8. John W. Blair, The Control of Oil, (New York:
    Praeger, 1976), and Edith Penrose, "The Develop-
    ment of Crisis," in Raymond Vernon (Editor), The
    Oil Crisis, (New York: W.W. Norton, 1976), pp. 39-57.

9. Joel Darmstadter and Hans Landsberg, "The Economic
    Background," in Raymond Vernon (Editor), The Oil
    Crisis, (New York: W.W. Norton, 1976), p. 19.

10. Edith Penrose, op. cit., p. 49.

11. Joseph A. Yager et al., Energy and Foreign Policy,
    (Cambridge: Ballinger, 1974), p. 237.

12. 91st Congress, 2nd Session, Joint Economic Committee, <u>The Economy, Energy and the Environment</u>, September 1, 1970, p. 25.

13. <u>Ibid.</u>, p. 33.

14. <u>Ibid.</u>, p. 51.

15. <u>Ibid.</u>, p. 84.

16. Mason Willrich, "The Electric Utility and the Energy Crisis," <u>Public Utilities Fortnightly</u>, XCV, January 2, 1975, p. 24.

17. (See William Rodger, <u>Brown-Out</u>, New York: Stein and Day, 1972, for utility influence upon electric demand and feasibility of meeting self-generated demand).

18. 91st Congress, 2nd Session, Joint Economic Committee, <u>The Economy, Energy and the Environment</u>, September 1, 1970, p. 81.

19. <u>Ibid.</u>, p. 24.

20. 91st Congress, 1st Session, U.S. Joint Committee on Atomic Energy, <u>Environmental Effects of Producing Electric Power</u>, 1969, p. 65.

21. <u>Joint Economic Committee</u>, <u>op. cit.</u>, p. 8.

22. Remarks by Joseph Swidler, "The Critical Path Between Energy Supply and Environmental Protection," 83rd Annual Convention of the National Association of Regulatory Utility Commissioners, Atlantic City, N.J., September 13-16, 1971.

23. 93rd Congress, 2nd Session, United States Senate, <u>Financial Problems of the Electric Utilities</u>, Hearings before the Committee on Interior and Insular Affairs, August 7 and 8, 1974, p. 455.

24. <u>Ibid.</u>, p. 31.

25. John W. Blair, <u>op. cit.</u>, p. 296.

26. <u>Public Utilities Fortnightly</u>, editorial,
    June 22, 1972, p. 6.

27. <u>Electricity and the Environment</u>, New York
    Association of the Bar, (St. Paul: West
    Publishing Co., 1972), p. 23.

28. Remarks by Joseph Swidler, 83rd Annual Con-
    vention of National Association of Regulatory
    Utility Commissioners, <u>op. cit.</u>

29. Garrett Hardin, "The Tragedy of the Commons,"
    <u>Science</u>, V (December 13, 1968), p. 1244.

30. Austin Heller and Edward Ferrand, "Low Sulfur
    Fuels for New York City" in John Harte (Editor),
    <u>Patient Earth</u>, (New York: Holt, Rinehart and
    Winston, 1971). Other studies which emphasize
    the chemical reactions and biological effects
    are Carnow, Bertram et al., "Health Effects of
    Fossil Fuel Combustion: A Quantitative Approach,"
    <u>American Public Health Association</u>, Washington,
    D.C., 1974, Arlan Cohen et al., "Symptom Reporting
    during Recent Publicized and Unpublicized Air
    Pollution Episodes," <u>American Journal of Public
    Health</u>, May 1974.

31. Larry E. Ruff, "The Economic Common Sense of
    Pollution," in Robert and Nancy Dorfman (Editors),
    <u>Economics of the Environment</u>, (New York: W.W. Norton,
    1972).

32. Lyle E. Crain, "Institutions for Managing Lakes
    and Bays," <u>Natural Resources Journal</u>, XI, (July,
    1971), p. 524.

33. J.H. Dales, "The Property Interface," in Robert
    and Nancy Dorfman (Editors), <u>Economics of the
    Environment</u>, (New York: W.W. Norton, 1972), p. 308.

34. Garrett Hardin, <u>op. cit.</u>, p. 1244.

35. Vincent Ostrom, "Human Fallibility, Political
    Theory and the Environment," <u>Policy Studies
    Journal</u>, Summer 1973, p. 211.

36. Grant McConnell, <u>Private Power and American Democracy</u>, (New York: Knopf, 1967), p. 112.

37. Gerald Garvey, <u>Energy, Ecology, Economy</u>, (New York: W.W. Norton, 1972), Chapter 9. See also John Esposito, <u>Vanishing Air</u>, (New York: Grossman, 1970), John R. Sax, <u>Defending the Environment: A Strategy for Citizen Action</u>, (New York: Knopf, 1971), and Richard Saltonstall, <u>Your Environment and What You Can Do About It: A Citizen's Guide</u>, (New York: Walker, 1970).

38. Cynthia H. Enloe, <u>The Politics of Pollution in a Comparative Perspective</u>, (New York: David McKay Co., 1975).

39. Esther Rodetti Schacter, <u>Enforcing Air Pollution Controls</u>, (New York: Praeger, 1974).

40. Clarence Davies, <u>The Politics of Pollution</u>, (New York: Pegasus, 1970).

41. Grant McClellan, <u>Protecting Our Environment</u>, (New York: H.W. Wilson, 1970).

42. James Ridgeway, <u>The Politics of Ecology</u>, (New York: E.P. Dutton, 1970), See also Ron Linton, <u>Terracide</u>, (New York: Paperback Press, 1970).

43. James C. Hite, et al., <u>The Economics of Environmental Quality</u>, (Washington, D.C.: Institute for Public Policy Research, 1972).

44. James C. Hite, et al., ibid., H. Wolozin, <u>Economics of Air Pollution</u>, (New York: W.W. Norton, 1966), Ronald G. Ridker, <u>Economic Costs of Air Pollution: Studies in Measurement</u>, (New York: Praeger, 1966).

45. Barry Commoner, "The Environmental Costs of Economic Growth," in Dorfman, <u>ibid.</u>, pp. 261-283.

46. Larry Ruff, "The Economic Common Sense of Pollution," in Dorfman, <u>ibid.</u>, pp. 3-20.

32

47. <u>Electricity and the Environment</u>, New York
    Association of the Bar, <u>ibid.</u>, p. 166.

48. Michael Kraft, "Ecological Politics and
    American Government: A Review Essay," in
    Stuart Nagel (Editor), <u>Environmental Politics</u>,
    (New York: Praeger, 1975), p. 147.

49. Lester W. Milbraith, "The Environmental Problem
    as a Political Problem: An Agenda of Environ-
    mental Concerns for Political Scientists,"
    International Political Science Association
    Convention at Montreal, Canada, IX World Congress,
    August 1973, p. 4.

50. John Lehtey and Stahrl Edmunds, <u>Environmental
    Administration</u>, (New York: McGraw Hill, 1973),
    p. 430.

51. Michael Brenner, <u>The Political Economy of
    America's Environmental Dilemma</u>, (Massachusetts:
    Lexington Books, 1973), p. 7.

52. Robert L. Heilbroner, <u>An Inquiry Into the Human
    Prospect</u>, (New York: W.W. Norton, 1974).

53. Robert Paul Wolff, <u>The Poverty of Liberalism</u>,
    (Boston: Beacon Press, 1968), p. 121.

54. Lynton Caldwell, "Environmental Quality as an
    Administrative Problem," <u>Annals of the American
    Academy of Political and Social Science</u>, CCCC
    (November 1972), pp. 103-115, <u>Environment: A
    Challenge to Modern Society</u>, (New York: Doubleday,
    1971), <u>Man and His Environment: Policy and
    Administration</u>, (New York: Harper and Row, 1975).

55. Charles Komanoff, <u>The Price of Power: Electric
    Utilities and Environment</u>, (New York: Council on
    Economic Priorities, 1972).

56. <u>Council on Environmental Quality, 1st Annual
    Report</u>, August 1970.

57. <u>New York Times</u>, March 23, 1974.

33

58. New York Times, Editorial, April 7, 1974.

59. Remarks by Russell Train before the Edison
    Electric Institute, EPA Seminar, Washington,
    D.C., December 3, 1973.

60. Roy L. Meek and John Straayer, "The Iron Law
    of Environmental Disorder," in Roy L. Meek and
    John Straayer (Editors), The Politics of Neglect,
    (New York: Houghton Mifflin, 1971), p. 240.

61. Memo from Alan G. Kirk II, Enforcement and General
    Counsel to the Regional Administrator, Region II,
    EPA, January 10, 1974.

62. Conversation with Dr. Edward Ferrand, Director,
    Bureau of Technical Resources, Department of Air
    Resources, CEPA, February 14, 1978.

63. Grant McClellan, Protecting Our Environment,
    (New York: H.W. Wilson, 1970), p. 38.

64. New York City Environmental Protection Admini-
    stration, Minority Report to the Interdepartmental
    Committee on Public Utilities, July 31, 1970.

65. Grant McClellan, Protecting Our Environment,
    op. cit.

66. Bernard Goldstein, "Analysis of a Preliminary
    Manuscript entitled, 'Relation of Pollution
    Mortality, N.Y.C. 1963-1972'", Health Research
    Council of the City of New York, Environmental
    Pollution Working Group.

67. Anne Kolker Freedman and Jeffrey C. Cohen, The
    Environmental Impact of Supplying Power to the Con
    Edison Service Territory: 1975-1980, (New York:
    Citizens for Clean Air, August 1975), pp. 4-7.

68. Minority Report, New York City Environmental
    Protection Administration, July 31, 1970, p. 12.

34

69. Minority Report, New York City Environmental Protection Administration, July 31, 1970, p. 21.

70. Minority Report, New York City Environmental Protection Administration, July 31, 1970, p. 21.

71. Ibid., p. 20.

72. Freedman and Cohen, op. cit., p. J-1.

73. Case 26309, Opinion 73-31, Public Service Commission.

35

CHAPTER II

DECISION-MAKING

The Usefulness of Studying Decision-Making

A useful way to explore the dynamics of political phenomena is to concentrate on the decisional processes of a political subsystem.* This approach provides a framework for analyzing situational and institutional factors, as well as relationships influencing the final choices of decision-makers. It also establishes the operational link between contemplated action and the goals of a decision-maker. "The decision-making process enables us to reinterpret the present structure of things

---

*Decision theory has been used in economics, psychology, sociology and organization theory to describe and predict behavior. See Richard Zechkhouser, and Elmer Schaefer, "Public Policy and Normative Economic Theory," in Raymond Bauer and Kenneth Gergen (Editors), The Study of Policy Formation (New York: Free Press, 1968), who develop a quantitative decision-making model to effect optimal choice. Discussion of cost-benefit analysis can be found in Robert Baker, et al., Public Policy Development (New York: John Wiley, 1975). In the field of psychology see C.H. Coombs and S.S. Momouta, "Measuring Utility of Money Through Decisions," American Journal of Psychology (71), 1958, pp. 383-389. In organization theory see Philip Selznick, Leadership and Administration, (New York: Harper and Row, 1957), Victor A. Thompson, A Modern Organization, (New York: Alfred A. Knopf, 1961), and Ayert Richard and James March, A Behavioral Theory of the Firm, (Englewood Cliffs, New Jersey: Prentice-Hall, 1963), and Richard Cyert, et al., "Models in a Behavioral Theory of the Firm," American Behaviorist Scientist, No. 2, April 1959, pp. 87-95 and James D. Thompson and Arthur Tuden, "Strategies in Decision-Making," in Fremont Lyden, et al. (Editors), Policies, Decisions and Organizations, (New York: Meredith Corp., 1969), pp. 310-330.

in the context of what we have known in the past and seek in the future."[1] In addition, subjecting specific theories of decision-making to verification by means of empirical data provides an opportunity to link decision-making assumptions with real situations while identifying variables, constraints, and linkages.

Definition of a Decision

A decision is an action taken in response to a problematic situation; it is both a conscious choice by an individual or group from among alternative actions, and the final choice in a process initiated by response to a stimulus. "Decisions can be characterized as the instrumentality, the organizational mechanism, through which an attempt is made to reach an aspired state of affairs."[2] A decision is therefore the link between the stimulus and the goal of the decision-maker. The process of decision-making - the steps leading up to the final choice - constitute the decisional process, which primarily focuses on the behavior of actors, constrained by situational variables, in the realization of some goal. The decisional process "...is the sum of the particular techniques, methods, procedures and strategies by which a given decision is made"[3] ...and that may occur both in the public purview and beneath the layer of public awareness. Situational factors may include political, economic, and social resources, political configurations, administrative behavior, interest group and political party activity, and information level.**

**An alternate approach offered by Richard Snyder, concentrates on the identification of actors and the interactive processes which culminate in a decision. See Richard Snyder, "A Decision-Making Approach to the Study of Political Phenomena," in Roland Young (Editor), Approaches to the Study of Politics (Evanston: Northwestern University, 1958). A decisional process may also be perceived as a problem-solving situation. See Harold Lasswell, The Decisional Process: Seven Categories of Functional Analysis (College Park, Maryland: University of Maryland Press, 1956).

A decisional strategy designed to cope with
response-demanding situations, is a mechanism which
enables continual adjustment to changing environmental
conditions and uncertainty.[4]   Once an issue reaches a
stage where action is appropriate, selection of
decisional strategy can be made. The strategy used
in decisional situations serves as a guide to action.
Strategies vary with perception of the time frame in
which decision outputs occur, with amount of change
sought and with evaluation procedures. Decision-making
strategies fall on a spectrum from "rational comprehensive" to "disjointed incremental."

The Rational-Comprehensive Model

The rational-comprehensive model is based on
positive assumptions about people's ability to behave
in a rational manner, in a way reminiscent of human
behavior in classical economic theory. The first step
of the decision-maker in the rational-comprehensive
type of decision strategy is identification and formulation of the problem. The decision-maker establishes
parameters for the decisional situation and seeks to
include all relevant factors affecting the problem.
He can limit some of these factors by adjusting the
time horizon of outcomes to be considered.

Once the problem has been conceptualized, goals
or objectives which are to be maximized must be
established.   The more explicit they are, the easier
it is to formulate plans for action. If there is more
than one goal, decision-makers rank them in some order
of priority, ensuring that objectives remain internally
consistent.

The next stage is development of alternative means
by which to reach the agreed upon goals. This is the
operational stage whereby plans of action are formulated
to satisfy desired goals.

Once alternatives are established and criteria and
standards for evaluation are selected, plans can be
made to maximize each alternative. Alternatives may
then be compared with regard to their feasibility,

38

probability of occurrence, likelihood of unintended consequences, cost-benefit ratio, and probability of error in calculations.

Following these predictive techniques, the outcomes of competing alternatives can be identified and the consequences of each plan evaluated with respect to the satisfaction of goals and objectives. A course of action can then be chosen which best realizes the intended goals.[5]

Advantages of the Rational Model

This model of decision-making encourages: (1) a choice of alternatives after careful analysis of a problem; (2) an explanatory rationale for the selection of an alternative; (3) direction for future decisions; and (4) the opportunity for implementing substantial change where it is felt necessary. The rational-comprehensive model of decision-making offers the use of creative analytic methods to shape and mold the future in problem areas where the past offers no guidance. "It is in these instances of really new undertakings where a system-analytic approach, in the hands of a skilled analyst, often can lead us to be very inventive in developing new approaches and techniques."[6] William Capron suggests that rational-comprehensive decision-making is of obvious value where either (1) innovation in approaches and techniques is called for, or (2) substantial changes in government activity are being contemplated, or (3) dissatisfaction with past programs leads to revisionist activity.[7] Charting new paths frees the decision-maker of past decisions, and the burden of accounting for prior mistakes. The rational decision, a result of careful deliberation, thought, and calculation, has the potential of achieving the highest utility function in terms of desired outcomes.

Rational-comprehensive decision-making provides opportunities to coordinate policies across different issue areas. By meshing decisions of multiple decision-makers, it enables an overview of interacting policies.

The rational model emphasizes the search for knowledge. It encourages the expansion of the limits of cognitive powers to meet the demands of the problem-solving situation. Gaps or inconsistencies in knowledge force the decision-maker to develop new sources of information and to utilize such knowledge in a continuous feedback flow. This is a pervasive effort to justify the final decision as the culmination of a logical sequence of ordered analysis.

Limitations of the Rational Model

"Limits on human intellectual capacities and on available information set definite limits to man's capacity to be comprehensive."[8] Critics of rational-comprehensive decision-making contend that human rational powers are limited. A decision-maker cannot possibly know all relationships between causative factors and sets of problem areas. Critics argue that this method is too optimistic about resolving problems in a system characterized by open variables as con-trasted with a closed system where relationships among controlled and stable variables can be established.

Opponents of the rational model also contend that a decision-maker's rational powers are unnecessarily taxed and excessive costs are incurred in the attempt to formulate all possible alternatives which satisfy a goal. This exhaustive search for the best alternative may take considerable time and energy, an unsuitable factor when decisions must be made within a limited time frame. This lengthy, complex analytic approach may not be worth the effort - especially in cases where a suitable alternative is discovered early in the analytic process.

Another area of concern is the position of values on the decision-making spectrum. Critics of the rational-comprehensive model argue that: (1) decision-makers have difficulty agreeing on which values must be maximized at the expense of others; (2) even when basic values can be agreed upon, there may be value differences about the means employed to achieve an end; (3) values are unstable, changing over time and causing preferences to shift in alternative situations; and (4) solutions to problems may overlap into other problem areas, and the satisfaction achieved for the sake of one value may jeopardize attainment of another value.

Lindblom argues that the rational-comprehensive approach is unsuitable for complex problems which have shifting and amorphous boundaries.[9] For example, a singular problem like inflation can be linked to others such as unemployment and education. Lindblom implies that such "problems" cannot be solved using the rational-comprehensive approach because of the interlocking of groups, values, and problems, which no single solution can resolve.

Another limitation attributed to the rational-comprehensive model concerns the ability to determine outcomes of all alternatives under consideration. Herbert Simon warns that the difficulty in attributing a particular payoff to each outcome is not only an insurmountable task, but omits the occurrence of unanticipated consequences.[10] Decision-makers cannot possibly know outcomes of alteratives when knowledge of causal factors is incomplete.

Victor Thompson concludes that the rational-comprehensive model is unsuited to decision-making in our society because "...it is receptive to undemocratic organizational forms."[11] Rational-comprehensive forms contribute to organizational domination of the individual, institutionalizing choices for individuals, routinizing problem-solving, and promoting overall acceptance of organizational goals. The system develops monocratic characteristics where "...goals and orders are presumably handed down from above."[12] According to Thompson, the rational-comprehensive model encourages organizational growth, elite decision-making, and uniformity - all of which jeopardize democratic processes.

The Incremental Model

Incrementalism

Since most decision-making in the United States does not conform to the rational-comprehensive model,

critics of it have sought to formalize a behavioral
model of decision-making. Such a model has been
called "successive limited comparison," "partisan
mutual adjustments," and, more generically, "incrementalism." This model of decision-making reconciles
the limits of man's rational abilities with the demands of problem-solving by setting more limited tasks.

Incrementalism directs decision-makers to examine
only those values which are implicit in the alternatives
being considered, and then only by comparing their
differences. "One need not try to organize all possible
values into a coherent scheme, but, instead, can evaluate only what is relevant in actual policy choices..."[13]
Rather than finding a choice which maximizes all values,
values themselves are disregarded if they are "beyond
present interest."[14] One does not choose or rank
abstract values but chooses among "alternatives that
offer marginal combinations of values."[15] It is difficult to gain agreement on which values are to be maximized because of: (1) biases of decision-makers; (2) the
shifting of values over different time frames; and (3)
the problem of each alternative involving diverse values
which are too numerous to calculate. Therefore, in
incrementalism one only examines values in which alternative policies differ. The choice of alternative and
value are made simultaneously; one selects an alternative
in which small increments of values can be sacrificed for
other values in a compromise solution. Hence, policy
examination requires only comparative analysis of
marginal differences in values - a task which is more
adaptable both to people's intellectual capacities and
to their access to reliable information.

Incrementalism allows problems to be handled in a
serial and remedial fashion, enabling analysts to observe
previous moves. The decision-maker focuses on coping
with problems in a continual problem-solving process,
rather than on solving them. The policymaker can thus
make discrete moves away from an evil without having
formulated an overall strategy or solution to the problem.
Problems can be separated into sub-problems, each piece
being the focus of a different decision-maker. No one
decision-maker is responsible for total policy output;
policy analysis is instead carried out by numerous

42

decision-making centers, and aspects of a problem may be dealt with at different points without concern for the complicating interaction of those centers. When conflicts in policy occur, they can be resolved through bargaining by shifting the problem to a higher authoritative decision-making level.

Advantages of the Incremental Model

Incrementalism offers the decision-maker a more manageable task. By focusing on small discrete actions, large mistakes can be avoided, and remediation can be made if adverse outcomes begin to appear. Results of past moves can provide a basis for present decisions, and minor adjustments can be made when new data is introduced. The chronological order of related steps also increases the level of knowledge, enhancing ability to predict consequences of decisions and actions made by other groups.

Unanticipated consequences of decisions are accounted for by the existence of a multiplicity of decision-making centers in a particular policy area. If one decision-maker fails in one of his moves, or is beset with consequences which were not predicted, the omission or mistake will be picked up by another decision-maker. According to Lindblom, this is preferable to allocating time and energy for the anticipation of every contingency.[16] Although there is apparent uncoordination of policy, "...a high degree of administrative coordination occurs as each agency adjusts its policies to the concerns of the other agencies in the process of fragmented decision-making."[17]

Incrementalism avoids the difficulties decision-makers experience in securing agreement over values since only marginal differences are considered. It allows decision-makers to agree on policies regardless of their personal opinions. Long-term goal aspirations can be ignored by decision-makers because incrementalist decision-makers adjust the ends to fit the available means. "Since the policies ignored by the administrator are politically impossible and so irrelevant, the simplification of analysis achieved by concentrating on policies that differ only incrementally is not a capricious kind of simplification."[18]

Incrementalists contend that incrementalism is
compatible with a social organism that is pluralistic
and democratic in nature.[19] Incrementalism is closely
tied to the pluralist notions of politics which originated from the work of group theorists such as Bently,
Truman, Latham, and Dahl.[20] Group theory emphasizes
that competition among groups provides the political
system with flexibility; policies reflect the interaction, reconciliation, and conflict of groups in the
political arena. The political process provides the
context in which groups can channel their efforts to
gain support for their positions. Pluralism as an
extension of group theory is also the theoretical under-
pinning for incrementalism. Policymaking in a pluralist
and democratic system moves in small steps, which is
compatible with democratic societies where political
attitudes change slowly.[21] "It thus meets the needs
of a stable society, where slow evolution leads to
institutions that embody the wisdom of generations that
should not be carelessly endangered."[22] It is, according to Thompson, "...the only form of decision-making
consistent with the group basis of politics."[23] The
system is accessible (as pluralism requires) because
it allows for present and future demands to be dealt
with in an orderly fashion, thus producing stability.
Decisions are small and remedial, and in the absence
of long-range objectives, values are downplayed. Problems
reach decision-makers through the interplay of groups
and are processed by a complex adjustment of interests
and by the unseen hand of the political system. "The
link between the practice of the method of successive
limited comparisons and mutual adjustment of interests
in a highly fragmented decision-making process adds a
new facet to pluralist theories of government and administration."[24]

Limitations of the Incremental Model

While incrementalists may offer a descriptive model
of decision-making, its normative implications are open
to question. Free of analytical responsibilities,
incrementalism can always be used by decision-makers to
justify inaction. Wildavsky in The Politics of the Budgetary
Process, justifies incrementalism because on a practical
level it works. However, Dror argues, "If it is accepted

44

uncritically, it can be very dangerous. Since it offers
a 'scientific' rationalization of inertia and conserva-
tism, it can easily 'prove' itself through self-fulfilling
prophesy" and block improvements in policy and policy-
making.[25]

Incrementalism offers no guidance and direction for
future action. Policy develops in a haphazard manner
as a result of multiple decision centers lacking comprehensive overview. Although incrementalists argue that
problems neglected at one point in the decision process
will become central at another point, such overlap is
not inevitable. In addition to overlooking policies,
it may happen that two or more policies affecting an
issue area may conflict and wipe out the intended effects
of a decision move. Incrementalists, however, are
optimistic about the successful operation of redundancy
in incremental decision-making, as this statement by
Lindblom illustrates. "In a society like that of the
United States in which individuals are free to combine
to pursue almost any possible common interest they might
have and in which government agencies are sensitive to
the pressures of the group, ...all values and interests
have watchdogs."[26] Nevertheless, redundancy is still
only probablistic, considering the success of articulated
interests included in the political process. Incrementalist proponents often use "straw man" arguments like
Lindblom's to explain why incrementalism is superior to
rational-comprehensive decision-making, but the positive
attributes offered by incrementalism can often be found
in other decision-making strategies as well. The following are a sample of other "straw man" arguments. (1)
Incrementalism provides diversity, and rational-comprehensive
decision-making does not. However, in the rational-comprehensive model, competing interests may well be articulated
and handled. The greater the number of alternatives
examined, the greater is the opportunity for expression
of diverse interests. (2) The incremental model is
based on a chronological order of successive steps, which
increase the level of knowledge, enabling better predictions of consequences for similar proposed steps.[27]
However, the rational-comprehensive model does not omit
from analysis the knowledge gained from recent policy
moves; rather, it can incorporate new data into the
assessment of alternatives. The incremental model has
more justification if past policies have been judged

to be successful. But if incremental policies have
not produced satisfactory results, subsequent dissatisfaction could lead to undesirable radical change. If
problems have been persistently overlooked, thus precipitating crisis situations, radical movement away
from some evil may appear to be the only alternative.
Ironically, this is just what the incrementalist wants
to avoid.

Incrementalism is likewise unsuitable in situations
where precedent is lacking and a new problem area emerges.
Where decision-makers lack a past history to use as a
basis for their decisions, policies must be innovative.
Incrementalism is then unable to provide direction for
decision-making. "Incremental change often does not fit
new problems, since new knowledge and quickly changing
conditions often make the past a poor, largely irrelevant,
and even misleading guide for the future."[28]

Incrementalism transforms means into ends. Emphasizing agreement and feasibility, these evaluational
criteria eventually become goals themselves. Success
is evaluated in terms of pragmatic standards because
there are no other standards by which to assess the
"goodness" of a decision.

Since it is unnecessary to reconcile substantive
goals with each other, incremental decisions may be
inconsistent with each other. The interplay of numerous
small decisions which are never comparatively examined
may eventually thwart even the most feasible objectives.
Incrementalism allows basic differences in policies to
remain submerged until failure is apparent.

Efforts toward reconciliation of interests do not
encourage the search and acquisition of new information.
Problems resolved through successive limited steps,
especially in crisis situations, allow decision-makers
to justify their limitations and constraints in attempting
to reach a solution. They therefore have a ready explanation for their own helplessness. Incrementalism frees
the decision-maker from the responsibility of identifying the causal factors of problems. Because a decision-
maker is never bound to "solve" a problem, "...he never
expects his policy to be a final resolution of the

problem."[29] A decision-maker is therefore not motivated
to utilize available knowledge, seek new information,
and actively deal with problems. The diminished role
of rational thought and analysis further limits the
capacity to deal with the environment. "Even if it is
true that 'the growing intelligence of mankind seems
not to be growing rapidly enough to achieve mastery over
the social problems, which the advances of chronology
create,' and even if knowledge is one limited way among
many for preserving reality more fully, nevertheless it
is also true that 'systematic reasoning is something we
could not, as a species or as individuals, possibly do
without.'"[30], [31]

There is some agreement among political scientists
that pluralism is characteristic of the American political
system.[32] Since pluralism and incrementalism are theoretically linked, then critiques and comments about the
pluralist model will likewise apply to the system of
decision-making it uses.

One frequent comment is that the pluralist model
does not recognize that certain groups may be excluded
from the decision-making process.[33] Their interests
will not be protected by more powerful groups which
have a greater stake in maintaining the status quo.
Given this situation, the attribute of redundancy - which
suggests that each group has watchdogs looking after its
interests, and that a multiplicity of decision-makers
will eventually pick up an interest left unaccounted
for - loses its potency.

Based on a self-sustaining equilibrium, a pluralist
society is, "...temperamentally and intellectually ill-
prepared for the task of strategic planning."[34] Incremental decision-making avoids planning, anticipating
that future needs will be taken care of when they are
brought to the attention of a decision-maker. Decisions
"...seem to be largely unanticipated consequences of
previous and lesser decisions made under pressure from
a great variety of circumstances and participants."[35]

Pluralism encourages incremental decision-making
because groups are left to reach compromises. The
government plays a brokerage role, regulating the process

47

of bargaining among groups. Groups then are unable
to take a comprehensive view of any problem because
they are pitted against each other in a bargaining
situation. Decision-making becomes means-oriented and
primarily concerned with process, rather than with content and the formulation and implementation of objectives.
Robert Paul Wolff argues that this phenomenon results in
decision-making which ignores questions of the human
community "...by encouraging a politics of interest
group pressure in which there is no mechanism for the
discovery and expression of the common good."[36]

With incremental decision-making, a decision-maker
is unable to define or identify problems unless they
are brought to the attention of the decision-maker by
organized groups or media. Government is seen as passive until problems are brought to it. This tendency to
wait for a crisis to occur before action is taken increases the likelihood that a crisis will occur. Then,
the characteristics of decision strategy are shaped by
crisis conditions.

Rational-Incremental-Decision-Making Dichotomy

The argument that political scientists have de-
bated concerning a rational-incremental dichotomy
assumes an either-or relationship between incrementalism
and rational-comprehensive decision-making. This is an
artificial dichotomy; the models are better evaluated
as points on a spectrum. Empirical decision processes
are seldom purely of one pattern or the other. Rather,
they are hybrids falling between the pure theoretical
models. The usefulness and likelihood of one or the
other of these models prevailing varies with the characteristics of the issue, the values embraced, and the
structure of decision-making in a given society.

Since both models have normative and behavioral
implications, it is necessary to distinguish statements
for improving decision-making (normative) from descriptive statements (behavioral). The latter constitute
empirical judgments and can be validated with survey
data. The former are problematic, for they offer
direction to decision-makers by defining the scope of
the decision-making process. The argument over which

48

decision-making method is preferable must be decided not in behavioral terms but with regard to which is more suitable for specific decision-making situations.

Where incremental-pluralist styles are relied upon, problems are identified as public problems primarily by action or communication from particular interested groups. Where rational-comprehensive styles are relied upon, formal institutional mechanisms for identifying the public interest and public problems may be established (e.g., planning).

There can be little controversy that the reason incrementalism describes most current decision-making practices is that decision-makers are forced by pragmatic considerations to respond quickly to crisis. With time as a constraining factor, they consider as few alternatives as possible.

Since decision situations differ, some decisions may be better suited to alternative types of decision strategy. "When results of past policies have been found unsatisfactory, or have become so because of changes in what is wanted,...incremental change is neither descriptive of actual behavior nor a valid normative model."[37] Where incremental policies have contributed to cumulative dissatisfaction and when new areas of responsibility are being undertaken, rational-comprehensive analysis may be more suitable. When long-term values require substantive action, incremental decision-making offers only ameliorative steps. However, in situations where stability and predictive capability are difficult to obtain, incremental decision-making may be preferable. Decision-making situations may even require both types of decision-making to be undertaken simultaneously to encompass both the satisfaction of immediate and long-range goals.

It is sometimes difficult to distinguish whether a policy is incremental or more encompassing without reference to its historical or decisional situation. Some decisions may be perceived at one time as having enormous impact, and later as being embedded in social continuity. For example, when the welfare system was

49

instituted in the 1930's, it was considered a radical step. Yet current welfare policies are generally questioned only in terms of efficiency. In fact, the abolition of the welfare system without some form of substitute would now be considered a radical step.

Even though incrementalists claim to have eliminated the necessity for evaluational criteria, decision-makers must use some tool to assess feasibility. Accurate predictions of feasibility rest on the reliability of acquired knowledge and the effective use of predictive tools. The more sophisticated these factors become, the more likely the feasibility criteria of incrementalism will be met.

The search process for alternatives can also reflect the continuum between incremental and rational-comprehensive decision-making rather than a dichotomy. In incrementalism, the search process consists of a comprehensive analysis of the marginal differences among limited recognizable alternatives. Decision-makers are not encouraged to search for additional alternatives. Herbert Simon's model of "satisficing" is one step along the continuum. He suggests that the search continue until a satisfactory payoff is found. If the process is time-consuming, Simon advises that the "satisfactory" quality desired be redefined. The "satisficing" quality is somewhat closer to incrementalism and more realistic, according to Simon. "...Organisms adapt well enough to satisfice," but they do not, in general, "optimize."[38] Yehezkel Dror, however, is concerned with finding an alternative which he calls an optimal choice, that is closer to the rational-comprehensive end of the continuum. He suggests that, "we should continue searching until we either find such an alternative or conclude that we can find no such alternative within the means at our disposal, in which case we must mobilize additional resources for the search or change our standard of "good."[39] Dror differs from the incrementalists because of the criteria used to select the good alternative. His criteria include: (1) high probability that society will survive; (2) high probability that it will be politically and economically feasible; and (3) continual improvement in new policies as compared with the past.[40] Dror's interest in improving public policy-making leads him

50

to recommend extensive surveys of knowledge, continual
follow-up in each stage of policy-making, and utiliza-
tion of cost-benefit comparisons as tools to evaluate
alternatives.

One function which all decision-making serves is
to relieve uncertainty, which can constitute the greatest obstacle a decision-maker faces.[41] One way to
reduce uncertainty is to increase the level of information. The rational-comprehensive model provides a
framework where phenomena can be analyzed. Research
and analysis of problems provide a data base which can
increase predictive capabilities, and Dror's optimal
model of policy-making emphasizes this role of information as a means for improving policy-making. "Policy-
makers' subjective image of reality must approximate
the aspects of objective reality that are relevant to
their values as closely as possible...," to bring about
the desired results.[42] Information-gathering techniques
are intended to refine and keep in perspective a true
image of reality.

The rational-incremental dichotomy is also trouble-
some when considering the degree of change. It is not
true that all incremental decisions result in incremental
change. It is necessary to separate the effects of
a decision from the way in which the decision was made.
The incremental model of decision-making stresses
stability as opposed to the rapid or large-scale
change possible in rational-comprehensive decision-
making. However, not all decisions made incrementally
are followed by minor changes in outcome. It is con-
ceivable that unanticipated consequences may maximize
the intended impact of the decision. Moreover, a
series of incremental decisions may have an unexpected-
ly greater impact in the long run, particularly as the
fragmentation of decision-making units and the multiplicity of decision-making centers increase. When taken
cumulatively, the impact of numerous small decisions
can be greater than that of a single comprehensive
decision. Conversely, a decision made as a result of
rational-comprehensive analysis may produce minimal
results. It is therefore, too simplistic to argue that
one form of decision-making is superior because of the
intrinsic worth of its intended impact.

As we noted in our discussion of pluralism, exclusive use of incrementalism may perpetuate the status quo by not aggressively attacking problems and, instead, relying on events to shape policy. By allowing decision-makers a passive role, this aspect of incrementalism is at odds with the dominant rational culture which emphasizes conscious, calculated, and controlled actions.[43] Michael Brenner argues that quantified technology and predictability are dependent upon the ability to effect such actions - an ability that is limited for incrementalists by their focusing only on marginal change. The incrementalist neglects "...the element of rational, conscious, goal-oriented behavior among the political objects of its study."[44]

Rather than build a case for either incremental decision-making or rational-comprehensive decision-making, focus should be directed toward reconciling decision strategy with the particular decision situation. Dror notes that one reason decision-making theory has contributed little to complex policy-making is the failure to discriminate among various kinds of decisions.[45] In crisis situations, where time and uncertainty are constraining factors, decision-makers have little choice but to fashion their decisions in small moves. Incremental decision-making is pragmatic and satisfies short-term goals. Wildavsky, recognizing the merits of the more comprehensive approach, deals with the defects of incrementalism by adopting aids and strategies to support decision-making. He notes that, in budgetary matters, "An incremental approach guards against radical departures most of the time, whereas agency advocacy and strategies designed to take advantage of emergent needs help to ensure flexibility."[46] Rational-comprehensive decision-making incorporates long-term goals into its analysis and provides a framework to deal with whole sets of problems. The use of more sophisticated evaluation techniques and information processing and feedback mechanisms is directed at making decision-making "better", minimizing the occurrence of crisis situations.

Case Study Analysis

This book describes two case studies involving similar actors in different decision-making situations covering a four year time span. Data provided by these case studies may be useful in suggesting relationships and propositions operating in one political subsystem over time, in this case, energy-environmental politics in New York City. Such relationships or propositions may be tested in other political systems as well. Data can also be used to explain sources of variation in energy-environmental policy in one political subsystem within a time frame or among different political subsystems in a comparative fashion. The use of two cases has limited predictive value, but the cases may provide the basis for developing hypotheses derived from real life situations. It may be that we can perceive the different decision strategies used by actors, to be influenced by their institutional positions and subsequently, relate these differences to their chances for success in their own terms. It is anticipated that such efforts will contribute toward more complete understanding of energy-environmental politics.

Decision-making is used as an analytical tool to uncover variables influencing a particular political outcome (i.e., roles, constraints, resources and goals). Decision-making can be thought of as a pattern of observable events leading to a decision. The case study provides data from which a type of decision-making can be located on a contiuum from incrementalism to rational-comprehensive by comparing the theoretical attributes of a decision-making pattern with the empirical data. The decision-making pattern can be thought of as a dependent variable and the institutional and situational factors which influence that pattern as the independent variables. An illustration would be a problem with unstable and uncertain technical factors contributing to many small adjustments, that is, trial and error, which would encourage incremental decision-making.

Political scientists have only recently employed decision-making as a focus for analyzing political phenomena. Aaron Wildavsky in The Politics of the Budgetary Process.

53

(Boston: Little, Brown and Co., 1964), describes the
decision-making process of budgetary allocations in
Congress by identifying the strategies employed by
decision-makers. He characterizes the budgetary process
as a series of incremental moves compatible with
twentieth century American politics. George H. Hagevik,
in Decision-Making in Air Pollution Control (New York:
Praeger, 1970), one of the first studies to consider
decision-making from an environmental perspective, used
empirical data from the field of air pollution regulation
and found that incrementalism was most compatible with
the existing political and institutional framework,
especially with regard to its bargaining aspects.
Hagevik attempted to devise additional decision-making
strategies that could be integrated with a decentralized
and fragmented political system. Charles O. Jones'
Clean Air: The Policies and Politics of Pollution Control
(Pittsburgh: University of Pittsburgh Press, 1975) is a
comprehensive case study of air pollution in a Pennsylvania
town directed towards a greater understanding of the
political process of policy formulation and implementation.
It constitutes an effort to place decision-making in a
public policy framework utilizing empirical data to re-
define current models of public policy. Another case
study involving air pollution is The Un-Politics of Air
Pollution by Matthew Crenson (Baltimore: Johns Hopkins
University Press). He uses the case study method to
determine characteristics of political institutions to
explain the level of community involvement in the issue
of air pollution in two similar cities. Drawing on the
work of Schattschneider as well as Bachrach and Baratz
in the area of non-decision-making, he concludes that
there is a non-decision-making process where certain
issues never reach the decision-making stage.[47] This
phenomenon, he believes, may be the result of reputational
power never exercised. Although the four authors men-
tioned above used decision-making as a focus for analysis,
their research took them in different directions, illus-
trating the usefulness of the decision-making focus.

    The identification of a pattern of decision-making
can be thought of as a behavioral analysis, while the
normative analysis is the evaluative stage. Wildavsky,
recognizing this distinction in the last line of
The Politics of the Budgetary Process, says, "The intimate

connection between descriptive and normative statements is never more evident than when policy recommendations are made."[48]

One can appraise the effect of a type of decision-making, such as incremental, upon the ability of a local government, for example, to deal with energy-environmental crises. Such analysis could include the effect of incremental decision-making upon the availability of alternatives and the recurrence of crisis situations. Other normative analyses might address the impact of decision-making strategy upon the satisfaction of long- and short-range goals.

Behavioral and normative implications of decision-making strategy are often indistinguishable from each other in the literature, which incorrectly implies that what exists is preferable because it is what people do. This is particularly true of incrementalists, who suggest that the presence of a strategy or method implies that a preference for it has been expressed (i.e., normative choice), and that the choice was a conscious one. But is incrementalism then a result of a conscious choice among decision-makers rejecting other strategies or an observation of decisional behavior? The subtle shifting from descriptive to normative analysis is misleading. It is hoped that this author will not make the same error, having carefully reserved normative discussion of decision-making strategy for the concluding chapter.

CHAPTER II

FOOTNOTES

1. Irwin Bross (Editor), *Design for Decision*, (New York: Macmillan, 1953), p. 2.

2. *Ibid.*

3. James Robinson and R. Roger Majak in John Charlesworth, *Contemporary Political Analysis*, (New York: Free Press, 1967), p. 179.

4. Bross, *op. cit.*, p. 1.

5. For further discussion of the rational-comprehensive model see John Lehty and Stahrl Edmunds, *Environmental Administration*, (New York: McGraw Hill, 1973), p. 416; Craig C. Lundberg, "Administrative Decisions: A Scheme for Analysis," in William J. Gore and J.W. Dyson, *The Making of Decisions*, (New York: Free Press of Glencoe, 1964), p. 23; George H. Hagevik, *Decision-Making in Air Pollution Control*, (New York: Praeger, 1970), p. 22 and Graham T. Allison, "Conceptual Models and the Cuban Missile Crisis," *American Political Science Review*, No. 3, September 1969, pp. 689-718.

6. William Capron, "The Impact of Analysis on Bargaining in Government," in Alan A. Altshuller (Editor), *The Politics of the Federal Bureaucracy*, (New York: Dodd, Mead, 1968), p. 205.

7. *Ibid.*

8. Charles Lindblom, "The Science of Muddling Through," in William J. Gore and J.W. Dyson (Editors), *The Making of Decisions*, (New York: The Free Press of Glencoe, 1964), p. 162.

9. *Ibid.*, pp. 155-169.

10. Herbert Simon, "A Behavioral Model of Rational Choice," in Irwin Bross (Editor), *Design for Decision*, (New York: MacMillan, 1953), p. 115.

11. Victor A. Thompson, Decision Theory, Pure and Applied, (New Jersey: General Learning Corp., 1971), p. 10.

12. Ibid., p. 11.

13. Charles Lindblom, The Intelligence of Democracy, (New York: Free Press, 1965), p. 145.

14. Charles Lindblom, "The Science of Muddling Through," op. cit., p. 155.

15. Ibid., p. 160.

16. David Braybrooke and Charles Lindblom, A Strategy of Decision, (New York: Free Press, 1963), p. 126.

17. Ibid., p. 165.

18. Ibid., p. 164.

19. Victor Thompson, "Decision Theory, Pure and Applied," op. cit., p. 10.

20. See the work of Arthur Bentley, The Process of Government, (Chicago: University of Chicago Press, 1908); David Truman, The Governmental Process, (New York: Knopf, 1951); Earl Latham, The Group Basis of Politics, (Ithaca: Cornell University Press, 1952); Robert Dahl, A Preface to Democratic Theory, (Englewood Cliffs: Prentice-Hall, 1965); and Robert Dahl, Modern Political Analysis, (Englewood Cliffs: Prentice-Hall, 1970).

21. Charles Lindblom, "The Science of Muddling Through," op. cit., p. 163.

22. Yehezkel Dror, Public Policy Reexamined, (San Francisco: Chandler Publishing Co., 1968), p. 144.

23. Victor Thompson, op. cit., p. 9.

24. Charles Lindblom, "The Science of Muddling Through," op. cit., p. 165, ff. 7.

25. Yehezkel Dror, Public Policy Reexamined, op. cit.,
    p. 145.

26. Charles Lindblom, "The Science of Muddling Through,"
    op. cit., p. 164.

27. Ibid., p. 166.

28. Yehezkel Dror, Public Policy Reexamined, op. cit.,
    p. 302.

29. Charles Lindblom, "The Science of Muddling Through,"
    op. cit., p. 166.

30. Reinhold Niebuhr, Moral Man and Immoral Society,
    (New York: Scribner and Sons, 1960), p. 50 as cited
    in Yehezkel Dror, Public Policy Reexamined, op. cit.,
    p. 301.

31. Aldous Huxley, The Doors of Perception (London:
    Chatto and Windus, 1960), p. 62, as cited in Yehezkel
    Dror, Public Policy Reexamined, op. cit., p. 301.

32. Roy L. Meek and John Straayer, "The Iron Law of
    Environmental Disorder," in Meek and Straayer (Editors),
    The Politics of Neglect, (New York: Houghton Mifflin,
    1971); Henry Kariel, The Decline of American Pluralism,
    (Stanford: University of Stanford Press, 1961);
    Michael Brenner, The Political Economy of America's
    Changing Environmental Dilemma, (Massachusetts:
    Lexington Books, 1973).

33. Theodore Lowi, The End of Liberalism, (New York:
    Norton, 1969).

34. Michael Brenner, The Political Economy of America's
    Changing Environmental Dilemma, (Massachusetts:
    Lexington Books, 1973), p. 16.

35. Grant McConnell, Private Power and American Democracy,
    (New York: Knopf, 1967), p. 337.

36. Robert Paul Wolff, The Poverty of Liberalism, (Boston:
    Beacon Press, 1968), p. 160.

37. Yehezkel Dror, Public Policy Reexamined, op. cit.,
    p. 145.

38. Herbert Simon, "A Behavioral Model of Rational
    Choice," in Models of Man, (New York: Wiley, 1957),
    p. 261.

39. Yehezkel Dror, Public Policy Reexamined, op. cit.,
    p. 178.

40. Ibid., p. 187.

41. Ibid., p. 15.

42. Ibid., p. 167.

43. Michael Brenner, op. cit., p. 23.

44. Ibid.

45. Yehezkel Dror, Public Policy Reexamined, op. cit.,
    p. 13, ff. 1.

46. Aaron Wildavsky, The Politics of the Budgetary
    Process, (Boston: Little, Brown and Co., 1964),
    p. 178.

47. E.E. Schattschneider, The Semi-Soverign People,
    (New York: Dryden, 1960); and Peter Bachrach and
    Morton Baratz, Power and Poverty, (New York: Oxford
    University Press, 1970).

48. Aaron Wildavsky, op. cit., p. 180.

CHAPTER III

THE SETTING

The characteristics of intergovernmental relations in the American political system, particularly proliferating government programs and overlapping jurisdictional responsibilities, affect decision-making patterns. The dynamics of federalism become especially problematic when local governments must implement national and state policy directives where they lack technical resources and expertise and where major responsibility for policy formulation rests with the other governments. The dispersion of governmental power weakens the regulatory function. Moreover, local governments are subject to intense pressure from groups whose influence would be diluted if the scope of conflict were enlarged. Furthermore, coordination of activities among different levels of government becomes increasingly difficult as governments have taken on additional responsibilities to deal with societal ills. The proliferation of government programs on all government levels has increased the overlap of functional responsibility already inherent in the federalist structure. In addition to the fact that many programs are competitive, coordination becomes difficult when programs are in the same policy area or affect the same clients. Programmatic policy-making on different government levels lacking preconceived patterns or goals often results in unmanageable, ineffective and wasteful outcomes.

Attempts to attack social problems, i.e. poverty, urban decay and environmental degradation, cut across state and local political boundary lines as well as agency lines on any level of government. Such problems are not confined to political boundaries nor amenable to piece-meal solutions. The multiplication of decision-making centers is also due to the increase in decision-making autonomy of administrative agencies which have increased in numbers and complexity. This has contributed to the narrow focus of each decision-maker and conflict among decision centers.

This chapter describes structural factors common to the two case studies. It lists the major actors and describes their jurisdictional authority as described by administrative and statutory regulations.

A decision-making situation is formed of structural and political factors which determine the parameters of possible actions. The interaction between structural factors, which act as either constraints or mandates, and fluctuating political variables, combine to form the setting in which decisions are made. The way in which actors respond to structural factors affect the decision-making outcomes. Structural factors include administrative procedures, legal rules and regulations, and institutional hierarchies with authority. Structure has thus been defined as, "...arrangements of specialized and mutually dependent institutions that have evolved as citizens of a society have interacted with each other to organize collective action for the solution of common problems."[1] Structural factors affect policy choices in several ways. Administrative rules and statutory regulations serve as prescriptive guidelines for action by decision-makers. The rules and institutions influence interrelationships between decision-makers and other actors, limit options, and determine agenda.

Political factors that shape decision-making situations include potential sources of power and power configurations, relationships to other issues and authoritative actors, norms and perceptions of the actors, and issue salience to larger publics. Political variables tend to shift more rapidly than structural ones, for example, with a change of administration to leadership which espouses a new set of values or programs.

The role of each actor develops from (1) the actor's perception of his or her own position in an organization, (2) the actor's perceptions of other actors, and (3) the actor's desire to behave in ways which conform to regularized patterns of interaction based on prior experience. The major actors described below include: the Environmental Protection Agency, the Federal Energy Office, the Army Corps of Engineers, the New York State Department of Environmental Conservation, the New York State Public Service Commission, the New York City Environmental

61

Protection Administration, the Mayor's Office, and
Consolidated Edison.

The Environmental Protection Agency (EPA)

The two cases discussed in this study occurred in
two decision situations which shared the same actors in
stable and similar roles. On the federal level of
government, the primary environmental actor was the
Environmental Protection Agency (EPA). When the EPA
was established on December 2, 1970, it took over the
responsibilities of other federal agencies involving
both air and water pollution.[2] Transferred to its
jurisdiction were the Federal Water Quality Administration,
renamed the Water Quality Office (WQO), the National
Air Pollution Control Administration of the Department
of Health, Education and Welfare (HEW), renamed the
Air Pollution Control Office (APCO), the Bureau of
Radiological Health, and those sections of the Food
and Drug Administration that had dealt with pesticides,
radioactive standards, and environmental effect aspects
of the Atomic Energy Commission, and some functions of
the Department of Agriculture.[3] The broad powers of
EPA include the setting and enforcement of standards,
research about the causes, effects, and control strategies
of environmental pollution, and assistance to states and
localities.

Prior to EPA's establishment there were over 20
federal agencies concerned with some aspect of air
pollution. (For example, problems of smoke control
were handled by the Bureau of Mines in the Department
of the Interior, while other pollutants were studied
by the Division of Air Pollution of the Public Health
Service, which was switched in 1966 to the Bureau of
Disease Prevention and Environmental Control in HEW
until 1968, when it was again transferred to the
Consumer Protection and Environmental Health Service,
under the direct jurisdiction of the Secretary of HEW.)
During the 1960's Congress passed a series of Clean Air
Acts recognizing the need for some kind of comprehensive
national policy to deal with the problem of air pollution.
In 1963, the first Clean Air Act (P.L. 88-206) authorized
the federal government to gather data on the health
effects of pollutants and to assist states and localities

in the development of control programs with technical
assistance and matching grants. The 1965 Air Pollution
Control Act (P.L. 89-272) granted authority to establish
air emission standards for automobile exhaust to the
HEW Secretary. The Air Quality Act of 1967 (P.L. 90-148)
recognized the need for a greater federal role in air
pollution control, and directed HEW to establish atmospheric regions for the purpose of setting air quality
standards.

A major goal of EPA was to implement the Clean Air
Act of 1970 (P.L. 91-604).[4] Section 101(b) states the
purposes of the Act: "(1) to protect and enhance the
quality of the Nation's air resources so as to promote
the public health and welfare and the productive capacity
of its population; (2) to initiate and accelerate a
national research and development program to achieve
the prevention and control of air pollution; (3) to
provide technical and financial assistance to State
and local governments in connection with the development
and execution of their air pollution prevention and
control programs; and (4) to encourage and assist
the development and operation of regional air pollution
control programs."[5] Section 107 gave EPA the power to
designate air quality control regions for purposes of
setting standards. Section 108(a)(1) gave it authority
to formulate criteria for pollutants designated either
for having an adverse effect on health or for whose
presence in the air was a result of numerous or diverse
mobile or stationary sources. These criteria were to
be "...an expression of the scientific knowledge of
the relationship between various concentrations of air
pollutants and their adverse effects on man and his
environment."[6] The Administrator of EPA must then make
known the effects of these pollutants on the public
health and welfare and advise the states on air pollution
control techniques.[7] Following that, the Administrator
must publish national primary standards (affecting
health) and secondary standards (affecting public
welfare) which must be met by each control region.[8]
These standards "...prescribe pollutant exposures that
a political jurisdiction determines should not be
exceeded in a specific geographic area..."[9] Each state
must (after public hearings) submit an implementation

63

plan, "..,which provides for implementation, maintenance, and enforcement of such primary standards in each air quality control region within each state."[10]   The same procedure was to be followed for meeting secondary standards.   Primary standards were to be attained no later than three years after promulgation of the national standards (with a possible 2-year extension if requested by the Governor) and secondary standards within a reasonable time.   If the Administrator disapproves of the State Implementation Plan (SIP) or if a state does not submit a plan within the established time limit, the Administrator may impose regulations to meet primary and secondary air quality standards. If violations of an SIP occur, EPA may issue orders for compliance after 30 days notice, or may initiate civil action.   If a state then fails to enforce an SIP and violations are widespread, after another 30 days notice, EPA may begin to oversee enforcement of the SIP.[11]   In the fall of 1973, the EPA administrator ruled that any change in a state's air pollution control laws affecting the maintenance of an SIP would be subject to EPA review.[12]   EPA considered that such variances would be subject to civil suits under Section 304 of the Clean Air Act unless they were approved by EPA and became an official revision of the SIP (if only a temporary variance was being considered by the state).[13]   The fuel shortage of 1973-1974 led to a number of requests by states for variances to the SIP's because of the scarcity of low-polluting fuels.   EPA stated that need would be an overriding factor before any variances could be allowed, and that such variances would only be temporary and based upon proof from oil suppliers that clean fuels were unavailable.[14]   All variances to SIP's were published in the Federal Register.

Federal concern for water pollution has a longer history than for air pollution.   As early as 1912 the Public Health Service (PHS) was authorized to investigate the pollution of navigable waters. Although a Division of Water Pollution was established within the PHS in 1948, most research and related activity was carried on by the states.   The 1948 Federal Water Pollution Control Act[15] gave the states responsibility for the establishment and enforcement

of water quality standards, while the PHS coordinated
research and technical information upon the request
of the states. The Federal Water Pollution Control
Act of 1970[16] directed states to promulgate water
quality standards based on a determination of the
purposes of water use and the development of criteria
for each use. The Water Quality Office (WQO) of EPA
has authority to approve these standards. The Water
Quality Improvement Act of 1970[17] further provided
that any applicant for a federal license or permit,
for construction or operation of a facility which would
result in a discharge into a United States navigable
waterway, must provide the licensing agency with a
certificate from the appropriate state water quality
office assuring that water quality standards will not
be impaired. EPA advised that it would override state
recommendations where state standards were lax, non-
existent, or inconsistent with the purposes of the
Federal Water Pollution Control Act.[18]

    Although Congressional action in environmental
protection seemed a victory for environmentalists, the
Nixon administration was inclined to sacrifice
environmental concerns for other interests. President
Nixon contended that the relaxation of environmental
standards was necessary to avert a serious energy
crisis.[19] He proposed measures which opponents of
environmental legislation had long advocated, for
example: (1) to consider the cost of pollution controls
in the setting of standards; (2) to eliminate the non-
deterioration section of the Clean Air Act (which
prohibits a region from becoming more polluted even
if it was safely within air quality standards), allowing
air quality to decline to meet those standards; (3) to
give the President broad powers to suspend environmental
regulations and to speed up the licensing of nuclear
power plants, despite severe potential hazards.[20]
Nixon also supported the proposals of energy developers
to establish new sources of energy in spite of environmental consequences, for example, the dredging of deep
water ports for larger tanker vessels and construction
of the trans-Alaska pipeline. The White House also
advocated postponement of the implementation sections
of the Clean Air Act and the continuance of strip-
mining for purposes of energy development.

The Executive branch, which supported creation of the EPA, worked hard to impede EPA's efforts to fulfill its mandate. EPA disagreed with the argument that environmentalists were partially responsible for the energy crisis. "The current energy crisis is now being cited by those who fear the future as proof that concern for the environment has already begun to ruin us. They imply that we must abandon all the environmental nonsense and use fuel any way we please."[21] Russell E. Train, Administrator of EPA, openly disagreed with the President by insisting that air quality standards would not be relaxed.[22] Train argued that no inherent conflict existed between solutions to energy shortages and protection of the environment.[23] Suggesting that the energy crisis was providing some with support to attack environmental legislation, he stated, "The charge that environmental programs will impede economic activity is totally wrong. It's just the opposite. It's environmental burdens like the toll on human health that are the real constraints on growth."[24] Unfortunately for the EPA, waning support in the White House for strong environmental measures ensured the EPA a weak start.

The Federal Energy Office (FEO)

Congressional response to the fuel shortage which occurred in the fall of 1973 was the "Emergency Petroleum Allocation Act of 1973."[25] This granted the President specific temporary authority to allocate crude, residual, and all refined imported and domestic fuel products.[26] In order to carry out the intent of the legislation the President delegated this authority to a newly created Federal Energy Office (FEO) on December 6, 1973.[27] The Federal Petroleum Allocation Regulations stated that fuel oil allocations to electric utilities would be based on the extent to which conversions to coal could be made, the extent to which utilities had complied with federal suggestions to burn coal, and the extent to which coal could be used more fully by those utilities already using it.[28] The FEO also said it would base its recommendations on the availability of coal stocks and the minimal levels of residual fuel oil reserves deemed necessary by the Federal

Power Commission (FPC) to maintain power supplies.[29,30] The FEO wanted as many plants as possible to use fuels other than oil, thus freeing it for other uses. However, in order to meet national air quality standards, many power plants had just finished converting their boilers from coal-burning to oil-burning. Although neither FEO nor EPA could force fuel conversions, if utilities were denied oil allocations, they themselves would be forced to switch back to coal.

FEO and EPA developed conflicting views over the issue of coal conversion and the allocation of oil. While FEO was responsible for meeting energy demands, EPA was concerned that, in the process, gains that had been hard victories in air pollution control would be lost through widespread use of high polluting fuels. The enabling legislation took notice of this conflict but did not resolve it. The Emergency Petroleum Allocation Act merely stated that the Clean Air Act could not be contravened.[31] The EPA argued that before any utilities were converted back to coal the utilities must be able to prove that emission standards would be met.[32] The FEO was responsible for directing fuel to areas experiencing shortages, but it did so without regard for the sulfur content of the fuel. The EPA tried to minimize the impact of high polluting fuels by checking fuel supply data of utilities and intervening directly in fuel transactions between utilities and oil suppliers.

EPA also advised FEO on the relative feasibility of conversions to coal, placing the highest-polluted areas on the bottom of the list. By March 1974, 44 plants were identified for short-term conversions. EPA recommended short-term conversions while FEO officials were more inclined to advocate long-term conversions to ease the fuel shortage. EPA feared that once conversions to coal were made, utilities would be reluctant to switch back to oil when the fuel emergency subsided. Pending legislation, which would have made all conversions to coal permanent, substantiated EPA fears that progress in controlling air pollution would be permanently abated if high-polluting fuels were permitted even on a short-term basis.

67

The Army Corps of Engineers

The authority of the federal government to issue permits for contruction on or discharge into navigable waters rested with the Army Corps of Engineers by power assigned to it in the Rivers and Harbors Act of 1899 (also called the Refuse Act).[33] Section 13 provides in part, "...that it is unlawful to throw, discharge, or deposit, or cause suffer, or procure to be thrown, discharged, or deposited either from or out of any ship, barge, or other floating craft of any kind, or from the shore, wharf...any refuse matter of any kind or description whatever other than that flowing from street and sewers and passing therefrom in a liquid state, into any navigable water of the United States,...whereby navigation shall or may be impeded or obstructed..."[34] The Act also provided that the Corps be required to issue permits prescribing conditions and limitations to allow the deposit of material in navigable waters. Section 10 of the Refuse Act required the Corps to issue permits for the construction of any facility on a navigable waterway.

In order to fulfill the aims of water quality legislation and the National Environment Policy Act of 1969 (NEPA) (which required an environmental impact statement for any action by a federal agency that would significantly affect the environment), a permit program was announced by the President on December 23, 1970 to be administered by the Corps under the authority granted it under the Refuse Act.[35,36] The original intent of the Refuse Act was expanded in 1966 to interpret "discharge" as not only impediments to navigation but any agent of pollution.[37] Moreover, it included environmental factors not necessarily directly related to water quality, for example, a change in water temperature as the result of discharges of heated water, and any effect on fish and wildlife, aesthetics, recreation, or flood damage protection. All such factors were now to be considered by the Corps in its evaluation of permit application.[38]

68

After the Corps receives an application for a permit, it is forwarded to EPA, the Department of Interior, the National Oceanic and Atmospheric Administration of the Department of Commerce, and the head of any state wildlife agency for comments. It may also be sent to the Federal Power Commission (now the Federal Energy Regulatory Commission) and the Atomic Energy Commission (succeeded by the Nuclear Regulatory Commission) if their licensing is required. Public notice of the application is made to state, county, and municipal authorities with responsibility for water quality. If EPA finds that a permit for a proposed discharge is not consistent with water quality standards, the Secretary of the Army will not issue the permit.

The environmental impact statement required of all federal agencies where proposed action significantly affects the environment applies to the Corps only where a discharge has significant effect on the environment involving other than water quality factors.[39] (Water quality is addressed in sections of the 1970 Federal Water Pollution Control Act).[40] The impact statement must: (1) identify environmental impacts which will result from the proposed action; (2) discuss protective and remedial measures to counter the adverse environmental impact; (3) analyze the alternatives and justify the final choice; and (4) assess the long-term impact of irreversible effects.[41] Upon receipt of the statement, the Corps forwards it along with comments received from other federal agencies to the Council on Environmental Quality.

Although formal permit power was lodged with the Corps, it was required to abide by EPA recommendations. This generated tension between the two agencies. The Corps, sensitive about its low public image because of a history of public works projects which showed little concern for environmental matters, tried to enhance its status by exhibiting visible attention to the environment in the permit program.

The New York State Department of Environmental Conservation (DEC)

New York State, in response to increasing internal demands and growing responsibilities imposed by Federal

legislation on environmental matters, established the
Department of Environmental Conservation in 1970.[42]
The Division of Pure Waters oversees water quality
standards of the state and the Division of Air
Resources is responsible for maintaining air quality
standards. In 1972, the New York State legislature
passed the Environment Conservation Law to,"...conserve,
improve, and protect /the state's7 natural resources
and environment and control water, land and air pollution,
in order to enhance the health, safety and welfare of
the people of the state and their overall economic
and social well-being."[43] The Law states that the
policy of the state will be to guarantee, "...that the
widest range of beneficial uses of the environment is
attained without...health risk, unnecessary degradation
or other undesirable or unintended consequences," and
to promote patterns of economic development which
minimize adverse environmental effects.[44]

The Department of Environmental Conservation (DEC)
is authorized to issue permits for any construction
on a navigable waterway.[45] Public Health Law 1230.3(b),
which specifically applied to steam electric generating
plants, was superceded by Environmental Conservation
Law 17-7013(b), which authorizes permits for discharges,
and Environmental Conservation Law 15-0503, which
authorizes permits for construction. If a possibility
of destruction to natural resources exists (i.e., forests,
soil, water, fish and wildlife), DEC is required to
hold public hearings before issuing such a permit.[46]
In granting the permit, DEC,"...shall ascertain the
probable effect on natural resources of the state."[47]
However, the legislation provides no specific allowable
discharge criteria for any particular existing plant,
but sets temperature levels for a specific type of
water body which cannot be exceeded. Consequently,
there is discretion in evaluating the impact of
effluents from any particular source.

The Air Pollution Control Act of New York State
was designed to,"...maintain a reasonable degree of
purity of the air resources of the state, which shall
be consistent with the public health and welfare and
the public enjoyment..."[48],[49] One of the duties of
DEC is to develop a,"...comprehensive plan for the

70

control or abatement of existing air pollution and
for the control or prevention of any new air pollution."[50]
As required by the federal Clean Air Act of 1970, New
York State's Implementation Plan for meeting federal
air quality standards was approved on May 31, 1972.[51,52]
The approved standards and criteria appear in New York
Codes, Rules and Regulations, Part 225. Section 2(b)
establishes a limit on the sulfur content of fuel for
stationary air emission sources at .3% by weight. The
DEC Commissioner may grant an exception to this regulation
for a period of up to one year, if an insufficiency of
conforming fuel is certified by the Chairman of the
Public Service Commission (PSC). A temporary exemption
can be issued for up to 45 days if the applicant forwards an affidavit to the DEC Commissioner stating
that he is unable to obtain the required fuel, or that
the health and welfare in an area is jeopardized.[53]
DEC regulations also allow it to designate a local
agency to act as an agent of DEC in implementing and
enforcing the state's air quality regulations. New
York City is the only locality where that delegation
was made.

DEC performed its tasks under the close supervision
of the Governor's office with little opportunity to
develop independent strategies. Decisions were made
on the highest level of authority after consultation
with DEC staff personnel. The first DEC Commissioner,
Henry Diamond, maintained a comfortable working relationship with New York City's Environmental Protection
Administration and during the period from 1970 to 1973,
DEC usually followed CEPA initiatives. This pattern
was occasionally interrupted when the Governor's
office had a particular interest in opposing current
CEPA objectives, thereby coercing DEC to support
policies it did not favor.

The Public Service Commission (PSC)

The Public Service Commission (PSC), established
by New York State in 1907, regulates the operations
of public utilities in the state. Its supervisory
powers include approval of rates charged to customers,
determining utility service area, overseeing accounting
procedures, approval of franchises, issuance of

71

securities, and testing and inspecting equipment.
In the area of electric power generation, PSC must
approve all new construction of facilities. "No
gas corporation or electric corporation shall begin
construction of a gas plant or electric plant without
first having obtained the permission and approval
of the commission."[54] Another function of PSC is to
ensure that adequate supplies of fuel are available
for electric utilities to operate their plants. It
can order utilities to reserve specified amounts
of fuel for emergency use. If a fuel shortage is
anticipated, the PSC can order an increase in the
reserve margin requirements or issue a certification
of fuel insufficiency.

Growing dissatisfaction with electric companies,
high rates and poor service created a public interest
in PSC's record of utility regulation. The press
portrayed PSC Commissioners as political appointees
who were incompetent and function as rubber stamps
for the Governor and the utilities. The expansion
of the Chairman's powers under the Rockefeller
administration allowed PSC to increase its authority
in areas relating to utility functions while it
enhanced the Governor's role in PSC activities. The
close relationship between the Chairman and the Governor
afforded advantages. Although the primary responsibility
of PSC is to ensure that the state is provided with
adequate electric power, the Governor advocated that
it be the siting agency for new transmission facilities.[55]
Since under this arrangement, PSC would evaluate any
environmental effects incurred by projected new
sitings, this naturally upset environmentalists, who
noted that Governor Rockefeller's support of increased
electric power as an essential ingredient to economic
growth, coincided with utility and PSC attitudes.
Critics doubted that a power agency could impartially
evaluate environmental concerns when power was their
prime interest.

The New York City Environmental Protection
Administration (CEPA)

New York City government has been concerned
with controlling air pollution since the 1930's, when

the Department of Health established a smoke control
unit. The Bureau of Smoke Control, between World
War II and 1949, became part of the Department of
Housing and Buildings, and then independent in 1950.
The Bureau had responsibilities which included the
licensing of all equipment producing objectionable
emissions and forcing compliance with any rules or
regulations requiring alterations in existing equipment.[56] In 1952, the Department of Air Pollution
took over these functions. By 1965 public concern
with air pollution in New York City induced the City
Council to undertake a study of air pollution in the
metropolitan area. The Council's report indicated
that New York City had one of the highest levels for
sulfur dioxide and suspended particles of any United
States city.[57] With mayoral support and public
interest generated through a series of public hearings,
the Council passed Local Law 14 on May 29, 1966. It
stated that, "For the purpose of controlling and
reducing atmospheric pollution, it is hereby declared
to be the policy of the city to establish and maintain
active and continuing supervision of combustion...
contributing to atmospheric pollution..."[58] The new
law restricted the sulfur content of fossil fuels
citywide to 2.2% until May 20, 1967, 2% until October 1,
1969, and 1% thereafter.[59] The Council's success in
stimulating public interest in the environment was
one of the few times the usually weak City Council
took substantive action on a major issue.

Part of Mayor Lindsay's administrative reform
program designated to increase efficiency and the
coordination of social service delivery was the
consolidation of functional departments into "super-
agencies." Department of Air Resources (DAR)
Commissioner Robert Rickles prepared proposals for
such action early in the Lindsay administration.[60]
CEPA was the super agency created in 1968 to incorporate
the environmental monitoring functions of the Department
of Water Resources, the Department of Air Pollution,
the Department of Sanitation, and the Department of
Public Works.[61,62] Its mandated policy goals were:
(1) to preserve the total urban environment and restore
those elements of the environment that had already
deteriorated; and (2) to consolidate those offices
dealing with aspects of the environment.

73

One of CEPA's early achievements was the proposal
for a more stringent Air Code to the City Council,
conforming to the stricter federal and state standards
for sulfur dioxide, particulates, and other pollutants
(i.e., asbestos, lead, and mercury). These recommendations were approved by the City Council and became
Local Law 49.[63] The Code expressed the belief that
each citizen had the right to air that was not,
"...detrimental to life, health and enjoyment of his
property."[64] To that end CEPA would try to, "preserve,
protect and improve the air quality of the city."[65]
The Code tightened controls on the sulfur content of
fuel used by power plants to .55% after October 1, 1971
and .3% after October 1, 1972.[66] Variances to these
regulations could be granted, "...upon presentation
of adequate proof, that compliance with any provision
of this code or with any regulation or order of the
administrator,...would impose unreasonable hardship."[67]
Such a variance can be extended for a maximum period
of six months, but the applicant must file a written
petition with the CEPA Administrator. If there is a
fuel supply emergency which jeopardizes electric power
supply needs, a variance may be granted for up to 45
days circumventing the procedural requirements of the
code.[68] CEPA's successful record in reducing pollution
levels in the city, especially of particulates and
sulfur dioxide, was primarily due to these restrictions
for the sulfur content of fuel and to the upgrading
of incinerators.

Being a young agency, CEPA tried to expand its
influence within the administration and to build a
constituency to which it could turn for support.
CEPA acquired a crusading, idealistic image, attracting
young people drawn to city government by the reform
policies of the Lindsay administration.

The appointment of Jerome Kretchmer, a lawyer
and former Assemblyman, to the position of Administrator
was generally believed to be a result of his early
support for Lindsay's mayoral candidacy. Politically
ambitious, he later offered himself for mayoral
consideration in 1973. Kretchmer's leadership differed
in style from that of his predecessor Merle Eisenbud,
who was disinterested in major policy initiatives.

Kretchmer, however, gave new life to the agency. He brought in six crusading attorneys and developed a public information department to generate materials and act as a conduit for information exchange with the public. He challenged any actions by Con Edison which would jeopardize recent improvements in air quality. He believed strongly that Con Edison ought to be subject to stricter regulation by the city.

Kretchmer worked closely with the Commissioner of the Department of Air Resources, Robert Rickles. Rickles provided Kretchmer with technical information, and Kretchmer gave his full support to DAR activities. Neither Kretchmer nor Rickles were reticent about resisting the pressure of anyone - including the Mayor - if CEPA interests were being jeopardized. They believed that a position of strong advocacy could generate concern and create a mechanism for public choice in environmental matters. Since no real environmental constituency existed, they believed one had to be created. They argued that political appointees (such as themselves) must create constituencies to support their policies, whereas elected officials already exhibit constituent support at the polls as a base to work from. Kretchmer encouraged the CEPA staff to form working relationships with environmental interest groups such as Citizens for Clean Air and Clean Air Campaign and with news reporters such as Steve Lawrence of the New York Post, informing them of CEPA activities and actively consulting with them.

The Department of Air Resources was responsible for enforcing the city's Air Code. When the leadership of DAR passed to Rickles in 1970, a turning point in the city's relations with Con Edison occurred. Until then, the city publicized Con Edison programs to decrease air pollution. DAR let Con Edison know it would no longer publicly applaud the utility's leadership in converting to low sulfur content fuels, nor would it continue to answer public complaints about Con Edison. Further, it would no longer intervene with other governmental agencies on Con Edison's behalf and risk being accused of having too close a relationship with the utility. DAR abandoned the voluntary industry-governmental approach (which had been encouraged because

of the unfeasibility of shutting down a Con Edison
plant if it were in violation of the Code) for a
stricter and more antagonistic approach.

CEPA depended on DAR's Bureau of Technical
Services for technical data dealing with the impact
of fuel on air quality and the monitoring of stacks
to determine emission impact on air quality at specific
source points. Because of its specialized function
(to gather information), the Bureau remained a step
away from the political debates.

A temporary component of CEPA established in
October of 1973 was the Emergency Energy Supply Task
Force, which was formed to operate as a "think tank"
to deal with the emergency fuel supply problems
projected in the fall of 1973. Its role was to
establish the facts regarding availability of fuel
oil, to monitor Con Edison's fuel supply, and to make
recommendations to the Administrator on applications
for variances to the Air Code. The Task Force
became the city's liaison with Con Edison and state
and federal officials. Although CEPA's overriding
concern was environmental protection, its powers
were expanded to include a determination of which
fuels could be burned by users based on an analysis
of fuel availability and on the impact of fuels with
varying sulfur levels upon air quality. CEPA's relationship to Con Edison took an abrupt twist, since CEPA
became for a period a procurer of fuel for Con Edison.

The Mayor's Office

The Mayor's formal powers with respect to the
environment include the approval or denial of permits
by city agencies, such as those permits normally
required for construction. These agencies include
the Department of Buildings, the Department of Ports
and Terminals, and DAR permits for boiler installation.
In addition to directing the evaluation of agency
permits, if the Mayor wishes, he can informally control
the policies and impact of an agency by means of his
powers of appointment and budgetary decisions. The
Mayor can also, by executive order, create new commissions
or committees to supplement the activities of CEPA or

create an alternative mechanism for environmental
decision-making. The Interdepartmental Committee on
Public Utilities (ICPU) created in 1970 to deal with
problems relating to public utilities, was just such
a supplement.

Mayor Lindsay, a Republican fusion candidate,
had received much of his support from a coalition of
independents, liberals, and parts of the Democratic party
organization. He was often forced to balance competing
interests to maintain his sometimes shaky political
base. His base also included support from the private
sector (i.e., banking, the media, and real estate
interests) which was needed to raise the large sums
of money necessary for mayoral campaigns. On one
side, advisors in his Administration, including Kenneth
Patton of the Economic Development Administration,
were fearful that industry would leave the city if
power shortages and poor electric service continued.
Patton warned of repercussions such as a shrinking
tax base and lost jobs if environmentalists had their
way. The Mayor's position reflected an attempt to
placate both environmental advocates and the power
advocates (the latter consisting of commercial, real
estate, construction, and labor interests).

While Mayor Lindsay allowed CEPA an opportunity
to formulate plans and programs, his reluctance to
follow CEPA recommendations eventually led to
resignations of key CEPA staff. During the subsequent
administration of Mayor Abraham Beame, resignations
continued because of disillusionment within CEPA.

Even before recognition of the city's fiscal
crisis, the Beame Administration did not consider
the environment a high priority issue. Under Beame's
leadership, CEPA experienced a withdrawal of support
and agency funds. The number of CEPA inspectors was
substantially reduced from 90 to 12.[69] There was a
15% cutback of personnel in the DAR and a 176 position
loss in the Department of Water Resources.[70] Due to
these factors, CEPA had less freedom to pursue its
objectives. The agency was more closely supervised
by the Mayor's Office, receiving instructions which
often conflicted with CEPA staff recommendations.

77

Although Mayor Beame did not associate himself with
environmental issues, he preferred letting CEPA
remain the city's enforcement agency rather than
permit the state or federal government to assume
responsibility for the city's meeting requirements
of the State's Implementation Plan.

Consolidated Edison (Con Edison)

Con Edison has had a long, notable presence in
New York City politics. One reason is that Con Edison
has a monopoly over electric power generation in
the city. Con Edison in its present form was created
from a merger in 1933 with Consolidated Gas and other
local electric companies. At that time, Mayor LaGuardia,
recognizing the potential power of a monopoly utility,
unsuccessfully sought to reduce rate charges to the
city by implementing a yardstick approach allowing
the city to maintain a few of its own power plants.
Con Edison, with PSC support, argued that this would
impose a financial burden on its operations, and the
plan was abandoned.

A second reason for Con Edison's political power
involves the city's interest that Con Edison remain
healthy economically. If the value of Con Edison
stock declines, increasing the interest rate charged
to the utility for borrowing, the extra costs incurred
by the utility would eventually be borne by the consumer
in the form of higher rates. Therefore the electric
consumer has an interest in preserving the financial
viability of the utility.

Third, Con Edison is the largest single taxpayer
in the city: it paid a total of $262 million in real
property taxes to the city in 1973.[71] When expansion
of PASNY markets in New York City are considered as
an alternative to Con Edison's monopoly franchise,
the city's interest in tax payments from Con Edison
(passed on to power consumers) dissuades it from
seeking change.

Fourth, Con Edison has links with influential
groups in the city. Con Edison is a major employer
in the city, granting construction contracts to

78

private firms. Its minority recruitment program has been a source of praise by minority leaders. Con Edison has also established ties to local community leaders. Representatives of Con Edison attend civic functions, and economic support is given to street fairs, concerts and other neighborhood activities. Members of the Board of Directors represent important banking, financial, and legal institutions in the city, reinforcing links among the economically powerful.

A requisite or corporate management is the projection of the company's needs and markets for the future, i.e., long-term planning. Con Edison has projected a 4.2% growth rate in demand for 1975-1980 and 3.9% for the 1980-1985 period. To meet this demand, Con Edison must allow for construction of new facilities, retirements of old units, planned purchases and large additions to load to make sure net capacity resources exceed reserve requirements. System planning is done annually for 5 year periods and cover a 20 year range as required by Public Service Commission.

This type of activity carried on exclusively by the utility, excludes the public. Governmental authorities enter only at the approval stage when they are called on to rule on the particular question within their jurisdiction.

The government lacks any overall coordinating mechanism for meeting electric power demands on a local or regional basis. The myriad of governmental actors may produce conflicting policies which inhibit the implementation of each.

In conclusion, Con Edison's political clout stems from a combination of the city's dependence on a single source of power, a coalition of forces supporting Con Edison policies, a close association with the city's important economic leaders, and the absence of city input into the decisions which affect the way electric power is produced and marketed in the city.

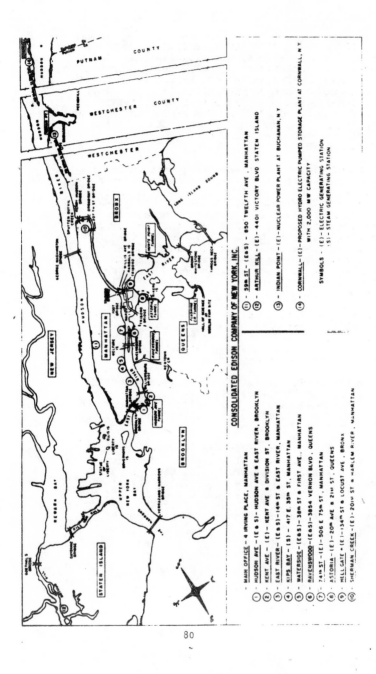

CONSOLIDATED EDISON COMPANY OF NEW YORK, INC.

- MAIN OFFICE – 4 IRVING PLACE, MANHATTAN

① HUDSON AVE – (E & S)– HUDSON AVE & EAST RIVER, BROOKLYN

② KENT AVE – (E)– KENT AVE & DIVISION ST, BROOKLYN

③ EAST RIVER – (E & S)–14ᵗʰ ST & EAST RIVER, MANHATTAN

④ KIPS BAY – (S) – 417 E 35ᵗʰ ST, MANHATTAN

⑤ WATERSIDE –(E & S)– 38ᵗʰ ST & FIRST AVE, MANHATTAN

⑥ RAVENSWOOD –(E & S)–3854 VERNON BLVD, QUEENS

⑦ 74ᵗʰ ST –(E)– 506 E 75ᵗʰ ST, MANHATTAN

⑧ ASTORIA –(E)– 20ᵗʰ AVE & 21ˢᵗ ST, QUEENS

⑨ HELL GATE –(E)– 134ᵗʰ ST & LOCUST AVE, BRONX

⑩ SHERMAN CREEK –(E)– 201ˢᵗ ST & HARLEM RIVER, MANHATTAN

⑪ 59ᵗʰ ST – (E&S)– 850 TWELFTH AVE, MANHATTAN

⑫ ARTHUR KILL – (E)– 4401 VICTORY BLVD STATEN ISLAND

⑬ INDIAN POINT – (E)– NUCLEAR POWER PLANT AT BUCHANAN, N Y

⑭ CORNWALL– (E)– PROPOSED HYDRO ELECTRIC PUMPED STORAGE PLANT AT CORNWALL, N Y
WITH 2,000 MW CAPACITY

SYMBOLS – (E)– ELECTRIC GENERATING STATION
(S)– STEAM GENERATING STATION

Conclusion

Structural factors were influential in limiting governmental decision-making strategies. The numerous and uncoordinated regulations required at different governmental levels and the absence of clear jurisdictional authority resulted in fragmented decision-making and a legal framework incapable of producing coordinated and continuing policy moves. This, in turn, increased bargaining requirements among agencies to reach decisions. Uncertain political factors (e.g. the competition between newer and more mature agencies) reinforced that effect.

The administrative and political setting established the fabric of interactions in which subsequent decisions were made. It was characterized by complexity and the fragmentation of authoritative functions. Crisis decision-making left little time for rational-comprehensive forms of analysis, yet without longer range perspectives, crises continued to appear in new forms. Piecemeal legislative responses, coupled with rapidly changing political configurations and the absence of long-range, comprehensive, internally consistent policy decisions, allowed for the continuation of an energy-environmental crisis.

CHAPTER III

FOOTNOTES

1. Lennart Lundquist, "Do Political Structures Matter in Environmental Politics," International Political Science Association, IX World Congress, Montreal, Canada, August 24, 1973, p. 2.

2. Reorganization Plan No. 3, 1970, Doc. No. 110364.

3. *Ibid*.

4. 42 U.S.C. 1857, December 31, 1970.

5. *Ibid*.

6. O.W. Stopinski, and R.P.V. Bakslertner, "Air Quality Criteria," in Robert Searle and Raymond A. Sierka, (Editors), Energy Needs and the Environment, (Tucson: University of Arizona Press, 1973), p. 149.

7. Clean Air Act, 42 U.S.C. 1857, Section 108(b) (1) (a).

8. *Ibid*., Section 109.

9. Stopinski, *op. cit.*

10. Clean Air Act, 42 U.S.C. 1857, Section 110 (a) (1).

11. *Ibid*., Section 113 (a) (1).

12. 40 CFR 51.32.

13. EPA Guidelines for This Winter's Fuel Problems, October 15, 1973.

14. Remarks by Russell E. Train, EPA Administrator, before the Edison Electric Institute, EPA Seminar, Washington, D.C., December 3, 1973.

15. 62 Stat. 1155.

82

16. 33 U.S.C. 466.

17. 33 U.S.C. 1171 Sec. 21 (b), P.L. 91-224.

18. New York Times, April 7, 1971.

19. New York Times, September 9, 1973.

20. Ibid.

21. Remarks by Russell Train before the Edison Electric Institute, op. cit.

22. New York Times, September 11, 1973.

23. Wall Street Journal, March 22, 1974.

24. New York Times, op. cit.

25. 87 Stat. 627, P.L. 93-159, passed November 27, 1973.

26. Ibid.

27. Executive Order No. 11748, 38 F.R. 33575.

28. 10 CRF Ch. II, Part 200.59 (b) (2) (1), December 13, 1973.

29. Ibid.

30. 10 CRF Ch. II, Part 211.163 (b).

31. 87 Stat. 627, P.L. 93-159, 1973.

32. EPA Action Memo, March 25, 1974.

33. 33 U.S.C. 407, Adopted March 3, 1899.

34. Ibid.

35. 42 U.S.C. 4321-4347.

36. Executive Order No. 11574, "The Administration of the Refuse Act Permit Program," 35 F.R. 19627-19628.

37. U.S. v. Standard Oil (384 U.S. 224).

38. Hearings held by the Army Corps of Engineers, March 24, 1972, Astoria, Queens.

39. Federal Water Pollution Control Act of 1970, Section 21 (b) and (c), 36 F.R. 6570, April 7, 1961.

40. 36 F.R. 6570, April 7, 1971.

41. 42 U.S.C. 4321-4347.

42. Chapter 140, Laws of 1970.

43. Environment Conservation Law, Section 1-0101.

44. Ibid., Section 1-0101, (c) (b).

45. Ibid., Section 15-0503 (1).

46. Ibid., Section 15-0503 (3) (d).

47. Ibid., Section 15-0503 (3) (b).

48. Environment Conservation Law, Article 19.

49. Ibid., Section 19-0103.

50. Ibid., Section 19-0301 (2) (a).

51. 42 U.S.C. 1857 et. seq.

52. 37 F.R. 10842.

53. 6 NYCRR Part 225.3 (b).

54. Public Service Law, Article 4, Section 68. As of July 1972, a certificate of environmental compatibility and public need from the State Board on Electric Generating, Siting and the Environment became a requirement. See Article VIII, Public Service Law, Section 141.

55. Public Service Law, Article VII effective July 1, 1970.

56. Local Law 4 (1949) and Local Laws 114 and 115 (1952).

57. See minutes of Council, June 22, 1965, pp. 1186-1258.

58. Chapter 41 of the New York City Administrative Code, Section 892-1.0.

59. Ibid., Section 833-1.0.

60. Interview with Carolyn Konheim, Department of Air Resources, Public Information, November 5, 1977.

61. Local Law 3, Executive Order, N.65, 1968.

62. Transition Papers, V1, Fund for the City of New York, 1974.

63. Chapter 5 of the City Administrative Code, passed by the City Council, August 25, 1971.

64. Ibid., Section 1403.2.

65. Ibid.

66. Ibid., Section 1403.2-3.11(a).

67. Ibid., Section 1403.2-3.11(a).

68. Ibid., Section 1403.3-1303 (c).

69. Stan Luxenberg, "Who's Enforcing Air Pollution Laws in New York?", New England, April 1975, p. 44.

70. Message of the Mayor, 1974-1975, Executive Budget.

71. Phyllis Peterson, "Con Edison (B)," Papers of Harvard Business School, 1974, p. 7.

CHAPTER IV

PROPOSITIONS DERIVED FROM CASE STUDIES

These two case studies were selected because they provide an opportunity to observe decision-making situations involving a conflict between environmental and energy values in a large urban setting. Moreover, they share common characteristics. One major actor was a private-sector utility with centralized management and clear objectives to increase power supplies and reduce fuel costs. The other major actor was the City of New York whose goals, considering the many interest groups and constituents it was obliged to consider, were multiple and shifting and whose powers were in effect shared with state and federal governments. The city lacked important resources which affect the range of alternatives that could be considered; for example, the city lacked independent sources of data and planned strategies to deal with crisis situations. In both cases: (1) crisis conditions forced the city to short-term action; (2) the uncertainty of meeting electric power demand represented a substantial political risk; (3) long-term goals were in conflict with shorter-term goals; and (4) jurisdictional authority was split among multiple governmental actors.

In this chapter, the author presents seven propositions which are drawn from the narratives of the case studies which follow each proposition.

The propositions which follow suggest (1) how the structure and strategies of decision-making affected the resources of actors and their success in a competitive bargaining situation, and (2) the influence of complex interaction among governmental actors upon outcomes. The first three propositions relate information resources to both authority of governmental actors and their powers.

> Proposition 1: Authority (e.g., licensing, setting standards, rate regulation, project approval) as a resource in the decisional process is of limited value if the infor-

86

mation resource is elsewhere controlled.
As the control of information by an agency
increases, the impact of its formal powers
also increases.

The control of information is a major resource of
decision-makers. "The indirect ways through which
power may be exercised include such phenomena as
controlling information and communications, thus
restricting what will and will not be considered by
decision-makers."[1] Where authorities are called upon
to make decisions defining the scope of an applicant's
action, information becomes an important component
of the deliberative process. If the authority lacks
independent sources of data and becomes dependent
on the applicant for data, the independence of the
authority becomes tainted and the applicant's power
to influence decisions increases.

Information allows the participants in a decision-
making process (the actors) to assess the external
situation and to place the decision situation in a
particular context. It provides a basis for agency
evaluation of the kinds of decisions which can be made
and the alternatives which are feasible. It enables
the actors controlling it to make convincing public
arguments. Its usefulness is limited when decision-
makers are prevented from assessing a situation with
accurate clues. The larger the number of information
resources available to an agency, the more opportunity
it has to judge the accuracy and reliability of competing
data. On the other hand, control of data outside the
agency limits this process. Control of information
outside the decision-making agency effects the choices
available to decision-makers and therefore affects
possible outcomes.

When an agency is unable to offer public guidance
because it lacks technical expertise, public involvement
may be inhibited. While public hearings may be an
attempt by an agency to gather information, it may not
have the intended impact because the public, in its
turn, may feel ill-equipped to debate the proposal
at issue. The technical nature of many energy/
environmental issues restricts the scope of public

87

debate because both agency personnel and the public may retreat from deciding a complex problem with which they lack experience.

In both decision situations under review, city agencies (1) lacked competing sources of data, and (2) lacked the expertise necessary to evaluate the data that was available. Con Edison was the source of most of the data acquired by the city. Information the government did have was dispersed among agencies with overlapping jurisdiction.

The Astoria Controversy

Background

Con Edison's proposal to expand its generating facilities in Astoria, Queens occurred at a time when public officials were concerned about electric power reliability because of frequent brown-outs and forced voltage reductions. These episodes however, were not the result of a surge of demand since New York City uses less electricity per capita than the nation as a whole. The city experienced a growth rate in customer use of electricity from 1960 to 1970 of 5.2% which was less than the national average of 7.4%.[2] Nevertheless, Con Edison estimated in 1970 that it would have to construct 2,700 MW of new installed capacity by 1973 and almost 6,000 MW of new installed capacity by 1980 to meet projected demand by New York City.[3]

In the early 1960's Con Edison had unsuccessfully attempted to construct a nuclear facility at its site in Ravenswood, Queens, in order to increase its generating capacity. Community opposition to having a nuclear plant in a densely populated area - which was, incidentally, across the river from the United Nations - forced Con Edison to withdraw its proposal from the FPC in 1963. Instead, Con Edison installed a 1,000 MW steam generating unit (the largest in the United States) and called it affectionately "Big Allis" since it was manufactured by Allis-Chalmers, Inc.

In 1966, while the city was establishing more stringent air pollution controls, Con Edison and

88

Mayor John Lindsay signed a Memorandum of Understanding, in which it was agreed that any new coal or oil-fired plants would be built outside the city. Promising to conform to clean air standards by 1976, Con Edison Chairman Charles Luce said that any new electric power that the city required would be brought in on transmission lines.

On July 22, 1969, Chairman Charles Luce proposed the addition of a 1,600 MW facility (two 800 MW plants) at its site in Astoria, Queens which already housed four generators with a total capacity of 1,455 MW. Luce claimed this proposal was consistent with environmental goals and the 1966 Memorandum of Understanding. Moreover, the construction was deemed mandatory if a power crisis was to be averted in 1974. In return for the city's approval, Luce proposed to use fuel with a .37% sulfur content at Astoria, which he argued would reduce sulfur emissions by 60%. However, Luce refused to consider the use of .37% sulfur fuel at all Con Edison plants unless all users in the city followed suit. Luce used an ambiguity in the 1966 Memorandum which stated: "Con Edison accepts the principle that, to the fullest possible extent, power from coal or oil-fired plants should be generated outside the city limits."[4] Con Edison argued that, although it had begun a program of construction outside the city, it still needed additional power because of delays in the completion of three of these plants.

In the Spring of 1970, the Mayor organized an Interdepartmental Committee on Public Utilities (ICPU) to evaluate the Astoria proposal. It consisted of the commissioners of four city agencies: Milton Musicus from the Municipal Services Administration; Jerome Kretchmer from the Environmental Protection Administration; Kenneth Patton from the Economic Development Administration; Bess Myerson from the Department of Consumer Affairs; and Timothy Costello, Deputy Mayor. Also included was Lee Rankin, Corporation Counsel, in an advisory capacity. On May 28, 1970, representatives of Con Edison appeared before ICPU to outline the proposed expansion. Administrator Kretchmer complained that Con Edison was reluctant to provide adequate documentation for the need of the Astoria plant.[5]

In a letter from Con Edison Vice-President Louis H.
Roddis, Jr., to Milton Musicus, Chairman of ICPU, Con
Edison simply restated its case. The delays on upstate
plants, increase of power demand, intention to retire
old plants, inapplicability of gas turbines for base-
loads, expense and legal difficulties securing transmission rights, and the unreliability of purchased
power, left the Astoria plant as the only alternative.
In support of its position, Con Edison referred ICPU
to FPC Chairman Nassikas' May 20th letter which
expressed the hope that "no undue delays will be encountered in accomplishing the installation of these
units on schedule."[6]

During the period of time that ICPU was preparing
its report, Con Edison suffered outages at "Big Allis"
in Queens. Numerous "brown-outs" forced the federal
government to make several hundred megawatts available
to Con Edison through the Tennessee Valley Authority.

Resources and Authority

In the Astoria controversy, the city lacked its
own resources to determine whether Con Edison was
correct in its claim that the city would suffer power
shortages without the construction of the proposed
plant. The city received little assistance from state
and federal power regulatory agencies which offered
only scant analysis. PSC approved Con Edison's 10-Year
Plan in November 1969, including the construction of
Astoria #6 and #7, but neither a separate analysis of
other alternatives nor any environmental assessment
of the proposal was included. The FPC suggested that
air quality standards could be met for the Astoria
plants, which were deemed the only available alternative to ensure an adequate power supply.

The inexperience of the city in regulatory matters
was reflected by its ignorance of its own powers.
Months after the project was under consideration,
the City Environmental Protection Administration (CEPA)
was unaware that it had specific permit powers which
could halt the project. Because of the lack of
evidence that the variance was controversial, the
engineer who received it handled the permit in a

90

routine fashion (permits were ordinarily handled by low-level bureaucrats). In fact, the matter had been handled so routinely by the Department of Air Resources (DAR) that it granted Con Edison a permit to install the new boilers without ever informing DAR Commissioner Rickels of the action made under his authority.

In an effort to reduce Con Edison's control of the decision situation, CEPA pressed the Mayor to open the controversy to public debate, to solicit additional opinions and to obtain more precise information in the hope of dramatizing the environmental impact of the proposal. One means to acquire information was to broaden the scope of the conflict to include more actors who could be sources of information for the city. Although the Mayor sought opinions from authoritative agencies at different levels of government, as well as interest groups and political leaders, none had concentrated technical resources capable of counter-balancing those of Con Edison.

The city lacked information about the feasibility of installing pollution control devices at Con Edison's plants. The city also lacked any means of forcing Con Edison to develop or install such devices. New York relied on the development of stack gas-removal techniques by Con Edison, which had taken little initiative in this area. Without its own research facilities, or input into those at Con Edison, the city relied on Con Edison's estimates of cost and feasibility for equipment which would reduce Con Edison's contribution to air pollution in the city. The lack of any authoritative power to force the development of pollution control measures or more efficient power production, together with the city's low level of technical knowledge, gave Con Edison no motivation to alter its present methods of generating electricity and consequently to decrease its environmental impact.

Although CEPA was poor in data, it tended to believe that Con Edison over-estimated its power needs and that the utility already had the necessary reserve power required by FPC. However, Con Edison maintained that the current power system would become increasingly taxed because of new construction, such as the World Trade Center. Con Edison contended that increased power demands forced them to take measures to even out the system for peak periods – necessitating the construction of the Astoria additions. CEPA was forced to use Con Edison's own estimates of current and projected demand figures to challenge Con Edison!

A primary concern of CEPA was to obtain information so it could perform its own analysis of the situation; however, most of the basic data was still produced by Con Edison. External factors such as inexperience, lack of expertise, and increasing political pressure hampered CEPA's ability to formulate independent analysis. If CEPA could not effectively challenge Con Edison's estimates of its power needs and the means required to satisfy such needs, the Mayor had little choice other than to rely on Con Edison's interpretation of the situation.

The 1973 Fuel Crisis

In New York City, the first sign of a local energy crisis appeared when Milton Musicus, Chairman of the ICPU, in a joint telegram with seven other northeastern states, asked President Nixon for mandatory fuel oil allocations to protect them against any impending fuel shortages. In October 1973, Con Edison announced that its suppliers could no longer meet their contractual obligations but could supply, at the same price, higher-sulfur fuel, which was forbidden by the City Air Code and the New York State Implementation Plan in that such fuel did not meet requirements of the Clean Air Act of 1970.*

Con Edison Chairman Charles Luce threatened that "draconian" measures would have to be taken unless high-sulfur fuel was permitted.[7] Con Edison asked the President's Energy Policy Office for strong federal leadership, including mandatory allocation of all fuels,

_____
*In a report on September 20, 1973, from Con Edison Vice-President Bertram Schwartz to Alan Roth of the PSC, Con Edison stated that the New England Petroleum Company (NEPCO) declared a force majeure but could meet obligations if they were allowed to pass on the higher prices needed to substitute Libyan oil.

suspension of sulfur restrictions and conservation measures (i.e., national auto speed limits, extension of daylight savings time, and limits on space heating temperature). Con Edison also suggested that the Federal Power Commission (FPC) remove restrictions on the use of natural gas by utilities.[8]

Con Edison Petitions the City and State

Con Edison's formal petition was filed on October 26, 1973. It requested permission to purchase, store, and use fuel oil with a higher sulfur content than that permitted in the City Air Code if conforming fuel was unavailable. Con Edison also requested a six-month variance from sections of the Air Code to allow it to purchase, store, and burn coal (with no sulfur content restrictions) at Ravenswood Boiler #30 and Arthur Kill Boiler #30, if residual fuel oil supply was unreliable.* Meanwhile, Con Edison contacted the President's office through FEO Director John Love, informing him of its intention to burn coal.[9] Con Edison wanted mandatory allocation of all fuel oils accompanied by relaxation of restrictions on the use of high-sulfur fuels by utilities. Con Edison's Vice-President Harry Woodbury explained to the city that suppliers were finding difficulty meeting their commitments because of Libya's nationalization of wells owned by Standard Oil of California (SOCAL), which he said supplied the New England Petroleum Corporation (NEPCO), Con Edison's major supplier. Amerada Hess Corporation, its second major supplier, also seemed to be affected by the embargo of Middle Eastern oil.

---

*Administrative Code of the City of New York, Chapter 57, Part II. Section 1403   2-9.07(c)
                                   "   2-9.09(a)(2)
                                   "   2-11.05(a)
                                   "   2-11.05(b)(1)
                                   "   2-13.03(d)
                                   "   2-13.09(a)(2)
                                   "   2-13.09(b)
                                   "   2-9.03(a)

About 60% of Con Edison's fuel oil originated in the Middle East and Africa. To offset any adverse effects, Con Edison promised to (1) purchase the lowest sulfur residual fuel reasonably available, and (2) enforce fuel conservation measures imposed by the city and state.[10]

Con Edison also had to apply to New York State for exemption from Section 225.2(b) of the State Air Pollution Control Code to permit the burning of high-sulfur fuel. In exchange for PSC certification of the insufficiency of low-sulfur residual oil and coal, Luce made similar promises to the state. However, Con Edison said it would use coal only when it believed adequate supplies of residual oil were unavailable. "Because of the difficulties and costs in estimating a coal supply line, we would anticipate the continual use of coal, once instituted, until the oil emergency is abated and that such use beyond the emergency does not impair the maintenance of ambient air quality standards.[11] According to Con Edison, the Ravenswood and Arthur Kill locations were chosen because of their high stacks, the short conversion time required (at Ravenswood), and the efficient electrostatic precipitator (at Arthur Kill). Luce, asked, however, that Con Edison be able to recover from its consumers "the substantial capital and operating costs association with coal burning."[12]

The Hearings for the Variance

With 12 days of public notice, the hearings were held on November 12, 1973, at 2 World Trade Center. They were conducted jointly by PSC, and DEC, with the federal EPA participating in order to maximize knowledge and avoid duplication. Bertram Schwartz, Con Edison Vice-President in charge of Fuel Supply and Planning, explained that the company was finding it impossible to obtain .3% sulfur content residual fuel oil because of the Middle East boycott. Amerada Hess Corp., which supplied 22% of Con Edison's needs, would only be able to deliver 1.2% to 1.3% sulfur content oil. Texaco, supplying 9% of Con Edison's needs, planned to reduce deliveries by 30% in November. Schwartz told the hearing officers that, even with the use of non-conforming oil, there would be a shortfall which

necessitated the use of coal at two of its plants.
Testimony from Leon Hess, head of Amerada Hess Corp.,
supported Con Edison's contentions. Hess warned of
possible shortages of even high-sulfur fuel if the
embargo were not ended. Con Edison also claimed it
could only obtain non-conforming high-sulfur coal but
would try to increase precipitator efficiency where it
was used. He explained that coal, if allowed, would
have to be used on a continuing basis. "The dis-
continuance of coal, once established, will be costly
to our consumers."[13] He admitted that there was no
desulfurization equipment at either of the plants and
that the precipitator at one of them was not working
up to design capacity.

   Government regulatory agencies were being forced
to respond to a situation where the basis of the
decision was information controlled primarily by Con
Edison or the oil companies. This limited the options
available to them and thus reduced their discretion.

The Governmental Response: CEPA

   Because CEPA believed Con Edison had exaggerated
the oil shortage, the city's response to its application
for a variance was more marked than that of either the
state or federal government. The city's estimate of
Con Edison's shortfall was 3 million barrels, rather
than the 4.2 million estimated by Con Edison for the
period November 1, 1973 to March 31, 1974. CEPA
appreciated the uncertainties owing to diverse actions
the federal government might take, as well as the
unpredictable effects of energy conservation measures
and weather conditions on energy demand. CEPA felt
it must take some action to forestall fuel shortages
because of the absence of any direction from Congress
or the Energy Policy Office. The city decided on
November 19, 1973 to grant Con Edison a variance (to
Section 1403.-2-3.11 of the Air Code) for six months;
in effect, to allow the burning of up to 3 million
barrels of residual oil exceeding Air Code limitations
for sulfur content. In return, Con Edison was to use
all possible remedies - including legal suits against
any supplier who failed to meet its contractual
obligations and report the status of those actions and
possible litigation to the Administrator of CEPA not

later than December 20, 1973.

The city denied Con Edison's request to burn coal at Ravenswood #30 and Arthur Kill #30, believing that shortages could be filled by non-conforming oil. Moreover, the city felt that the federal government was close to authorizing the switch to coal by utilities. (EPA had testified that the metropolitan area would be the last to convert because of its inability to meet ambient air quality standards.) By burning merely non-conforming fuel oil and no coal, Department of Air Resources Commissioner Fred Hart expected sulfur dioxide pollution to increase by 10%. Hart was also afraid that once coal burning was begun, it would be difficult to discontinue its use. "Our greatest fear is that once they get started, they will find some way to keep on burning coal."[14]

On December 18, 1973, the city amended its November 19th decision permitting Con Edison to purchase and store coal at Arthur Kill #30 subject to economic penalties (which were calculated at $6.50 per ton of coal which was supposed to equalize the cost of .3% oil). When the variance ended April 30, 1974, no revenues from these penalties had been collected.

During the month of December, additional hearings were held to ascertain whether the 45-day variances granted to fuel suppliers on November 19, 1973 should be extended. Oil companies testified that little conforming oil was available to the open market. However, the one exception was NEPCO, which said it was currently meeting its obligation for conforming oil and could continue to do so through the first quarter of 1974. Eight other companies serving the New York City area said they would probably not be able to meet their contractual obligations, even if they substituted non-conforming oil, because of the embargo. Hess and Sun Oil promised that if sulfur restrictions were lifted they could probably meet 90% of their obligations. Hess was granted a variance effective immediately for the period ending March 3, 1974, to "...transport, store, offer for sale and sell to authorized buyers...non-conforming residual and distillage fuel oil, but only provided that conforming residual or distillate fuel oil, as the case may be, is then not available in the quantity delivered..."[15]

96

Sun Oil was also granted a variance until March 31, 1974, for non-conforming distillate fuel oil only if conforming distillate fuel oil were not available. CEPA said that if other oil companies presented evidence for variances, their cases would be considered and temporary emergency variances could be granted. Hess and Sun were required to report to the EPA the quantity, grade, and sulfur content of fuel oil delivered within 48 hours after delivery, and offer a statement that conforming oil was then unavailable. The sulfur content of oil delivered to Con Edison had to conform to the restrictions of the November 19th variance.

Further Variances

Although the New England Petroleum Company (NEPCO), had not applied for a variance since November 19th, it had been shipping conforming oil to Con Edison after completing a deal with the nation of Libya that maintained its supply during the embargo. NEPCO transported its crude oil to Italy, where it was transferred to the Caribbean before shipment to the United States. Although the U.S. State Department may have had knowledge of this, the information was kept out of the public purview until it was "leaked" to the media in January 1974. Now Con Edison claimed it had a 600,000 barrel shortfall from NEPCO, which they said represented a 4-day drop in its reserve. Con Edison Vice-President Harry Woodbury notified EPA on January 4, 1974, that NEPCO had informed Con Edison that they would experience a 90% shortfall for January.[16] However, NEPCO said it would be able to supply the missing 90% after January 2, 1974. Con Edison claimed it had received neither a delivery schedule from NEPCO nor any of its January allocation.[17] CEPA staffer Larry Chertoff was also unable to find out what the conforming and non-conforming delivery schedule would be from NEPCO. CEPA then asked both Con Edison and NEPCO for a written explanation of the supply situation. Con Edison told the city that, as of January 8, 1974, 133,000 barrels had been delivered and that another 150,000 were scheduled for a January 14th delivery. It was later discovered that on January 8th NEPCO delivered 50,000 barrels of non-conforming 1.9% sulfur oil, even though NEPCO held no variance permitting the delivery of non-conforming fuel.

97

The city now had to play catch-up to obtain
compliance with its regulations. The legitimacy of city
authority was being eroded as conflicting data on the
fuel situation emerged. The major private sector actors
were writing the lines and the city found out only
after the play had already begun. This put the public
sector actors in the very difficult position of having
to determine the extent of the crises before it would
take proper action - and the data necessary to make that
determination was controlled by the private sector.

These matters were the subject of a meeting held
January 9th, attended by CEPA, DEC, and NEPCO. Neither
Edwin Carey, President of NEPCO (and brother of New York
State Governor Hugh Carey), nor Richard Weinart,
Executive Vice-President of NEPCO, were able to be
present. Norman Schneiderhan, NEPCO regional Sales
Manager, was sent instead. After arriving 1½ hours late,
he was unable to provide either information about the
status of the Bahamas refinery, which NEPCO claimed to
have been in trouble, or any explanation for NEPCO's
difficulty in meeting its contractual obligations.
CEPA felt he had been sent precisely because his position
as sales manager was unrelated to the issues that were
being investigated.[18] The result of the meeting was that
the city informed NEPCO of its sulfur violation and
requested an affidavit explaining its occurence and an
application for a variance.

On January 10, 1974, Carey confirmed the deliveries
of non-conforming oil to Con Edison on January 1st,
5th and 8th. NEPCO formally submitted an application
for a variance on January 22nd which, although promulgated
on February 11th, was backdated to January 11th. The
reasons set forth for this action in the variance
included NEPCO's difficulty in keeping its commitments because of its embargoed sources, and the
fact that NEPCO was a major supplier to Con Edison
as well as to residential and industrial consumers.
Con Edison could receive up to 300,000 barrels of
non-conforming oil during the period of the variance.
(The sulfur limitation was 1.5% as had been adopted
in the DEC variance.) A variance made on behalf of
Con Edison on February 11th - for non-conforming oil
over the 3 million barrels permitted in the November 19th
variance-allowed the additional use of 300,000 barrels

98

of non-conforming oil. CEPA noted that the application for this variance was not received until January 30, 1974 after delivery of the oil had been made, and that Con Edison could be liable for civil penalties pursuant to Air Code regulations.[19] The variance also required Con Edison to "install and maintain in good operating condition such devices and apparatus as the Administrator shall reasonably require in order to monitor and record the emission of sulfur and sulfur products from Con Edison generating facility stacks."[20] Although Con Edison assured the city that it would request variances sooner in the future,[21] the city had no choice but to comply with Con Edison's request because it had little lead time to confirm the utility's estimate of the fuel supply situation.

These events demonstrate the disadvantageous position of the city as compared to the private sector actors. Because the oil companies controlled the supply of oil and did not share supply figures with the regulatory agencies, the authority of the government was limited, e.g., NEPCO was able to supply non-conforming fuel without the knowledge of public officials forcing the granting of a variance after the fact when the action was inadvertantly discovered.

Data Resources

Of CEPA personnel interviewed, all agreed that the greatest problem encountered was the overwhelming lack of information. Con Edison supplied data to the city concerning its fuel needs, but the city had no way to judge whether such data was accurate. CEPA lacked the technical capability for analyzing fuel availability and supply data, analyses which were often lengthy and complex.

Although assessments of the severity of the fuel crisis were essentially based on the same data provided by the oil companies and Con Edison, each set of actors had a different perception of the situation. CEPA estimates of Con Edison's shortfall (supplies that must be committed to meet projected demand) was 2.3 million barrels, or 15,000 barrels per day for the period of the proposed variance, while Con Edison claimed the shortfall for the same period was 35,000 barrels per day.[22]

99

Lacking a reliable reporting system, it was difficult
for CEPA's Emergency Energy Supply Task Force to give
particular credence to a piece of information provided
by either the oil companies, Con Edison, or interest
groups. For example, Hess Oil testimony at hearings
in March 1974 concerning the availability of conforming
oil, could not be held reliable because Hess did not
have absolute control over its supplies, often purchasing
oil from other suppliers.

Although the media reported that the fuel situation
was stabilizing and that Con Edison's reserve capacity
had increased from 8.5 to 20 days supply during the
winter months, Con Edison continued to press for the
use of higher-sulfur fuels during February.[23] The
utility claimed that its suppliers were still unable
to meet their contractual obligations and that the
spot market for oil was unreliable. Because of the
embargo, NEPCO told Con Edison that low sulfur oil
from Libya was now unavailable, but it could continue
to supply 1% sulfur Nigerian oil.[24] Texaco had informed
Con Edison that it had sufficient quantities of high-
sulfur fuel available and that a further variance would
provide flexibility.[25] Exxon said they would have conforming oil available subject to the new petroleum allocation
regulations.[26] Hess told Con Edison they would be able
to resume delivery of conforming oil as of March 10, 1974.[27]
Con Edison interpreted this situation bleakly and
petitioned the city February 25 for a six-month variance
from the New York City Air Code to use non-conforming
residual fuel beginning March 28, and to purchase,
store, and use in the city coal with a sulfur content
greater than allowed in the present Code.

Application for a Variance Extension

Con Edison also applied to the state for exception
from the sulfur limitations of 6 NYCRR, Section 225.2,
and for permission to burn coal at Ravenswood and Arthur
Kill. It was determined by state and city officials
that a joint hearing would be the most efficient way
to deal with these applications, and an announcement
was made that they would take place March 14, 1974,
at 2 World Trade Center. At the hearings, Con Edison
would be asked to provide information on its ability
to purchase power, the progress made in enforcing

contracts with suppliers that had failed to deliver
committed quantities of fuel, results of federal
allocation policies, status in installation of
desulfurization equipment, precipitator efficiency
at sites where coal was contemplated, and results of
conservation efforts.

At this juncture, the informational resources
of the public sector actors had improved, enabling
them to challenge Con Edison with alternative
interpretations of Con Edison's own data. With the
availability of new information, CEPA was able to
challenge Con Edison's contention that the use of
coal was practical or desirable. Con Edison argued
that air quality had not deteriorated during the fuel
emergency and the use of coal would add only an
insignificant amount of particulates to the air
because of precipitator efficiency. Coal was considered
by Con Edison to be a good alternative because of its
price advantage and insignificant impact on air quality.

Under questioning by Jeffrey Cohen, President,
Citizens for Clean Air, Schwartz admitted that Con
Edison had underestimated its firm purchases of power
as well as the price of coal (which would make coal
less attractive and unnecessary). Schwartz said his
corporation was not asking for coal at the Astoria
plants because its stacks were low - which proved, he
said, that money was not Con Edison's only consideration.

There was additional disagreement over the extent
of the impact of higher-sulfur fuel on air quality.
In November of 1973, it was difficult to predict the
environmental impact because the sulfur level of the
fuel that would be available was not known. By the
March 1974 public hearings, both DAR and Con Edison
presented more detailed testimony on the impact upon
air quality, and although they both used a similar
data base, they each arrived at different conclusions.
Peter Freudenthal, Chief of the Air Engineering
Division of Con Edison, used statistics showing the
impact upon the annual average of sulfur dioxide.
Since the variance for coal was to be of six months
duration, the overall effect of additional Con Edison
pollution appeared numerically small. The annual
average SO_2 concentration was .002 to .004 ppm.

101

Dr. Edward Ferrand of DAR projected the number of tons of sulfur dioxide which would be released into the atmosphere to be a more substantial figure. DAR calculated that, if Ravenswood converted to coal and 1.25% sulfur oil, the annual emissions of SO_2 would increase from 12,194 tons to 61,087 tons, and the annual emissions of particulates would increase from 434 tons to 2,480 tons, assuming a 99% precipitator efficiency. If Arthur Kill converted to similar fuel, the annual emissions of SO_2 would increase from 5,291 tons to 26,770 tons, and the annual emissions of particulates would increase from 188 tons to 9,750 tons, assuming a 90% precipitator efficiency.[28] When looked at from this perspective, there is a more dramatic impact on air quality.

DAR noted that Con Edison did not show whether the 24-hour standard would be exceeded, but showed only a percentage increase. DAR believed the short-term impact was more significant than the annual average and asked Con Edison to clarify its figures and indicate the extent to which the 24-hour standard would be violated.

Charles Komanoff, CEPA, drew up figures for the emission impact of tons per day for SO_2 and particulates, which dramatized the short-range impact. According to Komanoff, using .3% sulfur fuel oil at Arthur Kill, there would be 14 tons per day of SO_2 and .51 tons per day of particulates. For Ravenswood #3 the figures are 17.460 tons per day and .67 tons per day, respectively.[29] Levels of precipitator efficiency has a significant effect on the level of emissions. Thus if during the time of the variance, precipitator efficiency were reduced, the city would have no way of controlling the environmental impact from the use of coal. Con Edison's precipitators at Ravenswood and Arthur Kill had not been tested since 1972.[30] The cost for upgrading the precipitator at Arthur Kill #3 which was not operating at the highest possible level of efficiency, would be substantial; Con Edison did not appear willing to undertake such an investment without guarantees that coal would be used for a substantial period of time. Unfortunately, Con Edison's precipitators had a history of breakdowns, and the city had to consider the consequences of this possibility.

By the March 1974 hearings, CEPA was in a better position to use the hearings for purposes of clarification and analysis of Con Edison's application for a variance. Con Edison had claimed in the past that the use of high stacks at Ravenswood and Arthur Kill would aid in the dispersion of emissions, and would produce smaller contributions of particulates in the immediate impact area. DAR challenged this contention, believing that the longer the gases were in the high stacks, the greater was the possibility that harmful sulfates would be formed, which are more dangerous than either SO_2 or particulates alone. Lacking EPA published standards for sulfates, DAR had difficulty estimating exactly what constituted safe levels. At the March hearings, DAR asked Freudenthal to provide additional data on this subject; the substance of the somewhat irrelevant response was that the largest source of sulfates was the breaking of ocean waves! [31]

Another dispute over facts which occurred at the March hearing concerned particulate emissions. Jeff Cohen, Citizens for Clean Air, discovered that in spite of a Con Edison projection that the annual average for particulates would be 1.7 micrograms per cubic meter, it was actually 3 micrograms per cubic meter. Freudenthal explained that the earlier projection assumed the fuel burned at Astoria had a lower sulfur content than later estimates. This example highlights one of the problems that CEPA encountered - the difficulty of estimating the impact of fuel on air quality when the sulfur level was unknown, largely because data on fuel availability and supply was lacking.

The hearings did offer some useful and surprising information when the oil companies announced the availability of oil, contrary to the testimony of Con Edison. Hess said it had been supplying 90% of its commitments and was currently supplying conforming oil to Con Edison. They took issue with Con Edison's estimate of the price differential between coal and oil, noting that the price of oil was declining. NEPCO testified that two-thirds of their FEO allocation of 1.3 million barrels would be conforming oil because of the resumption of Libyan oil stockpiling and the construction of a hydro-desulfurizer in Grand Bahama.

103

In an effort to develop their own information base, the environmental agencies took extraordinary measures. They confronted the oil suppliers directly for estimates of conforming and non-conforming fuel oil when the Emergency Energy Supply Task Force was unable to obtain the information from Con Edison. The Task Force also called upon the oil companies to learn of the possibilities of spot purchases, the information to be forwarded to Con Edison. (When Con Edison claimed it was unable to obtain low sulfur coal, Task Force staffer, Sally Streiter provided such a list of sources to them.)

EPA Deputy Regional Administrator Eric Outwater personally contacted NEPCO President Ed Carey in January 1974 to determine the extent of NEPCO's supply shortage, which would affect its commitments to Con Edison. The Emergency Energy Supply Task Force consulted with John Lichtblau of the Petroleum Industry Research Foundation (an occasional consultant for PSC), and with Jeff Bye of Shell Oil to obtain information of current prices and supplies. The Task Force called the coal companies to verify Con Edison's price estimates and discovered that coal was not as cheap as Con Edison had led them to believe. Even the Coast Guard was contacted in an effort to identify which tankers were in the harbor and their destination. Although as a condition to the November variance, Con Edison was required to make monthly reports, EPA Regional Administrator Gerald Hansler stated that EPA was not satisfied with their quality; in order to keep closer scrutiny of the situation, he asked Luce to provide weekly reports on the fuel supply situation.[32] DEC was also dissatisfied with Con Edison's report on flue gas desulfurization required by the November variance. Con Edison had asked for an extension of time for the report, which was barely met; and the report shed little new light on the subject.[33]

Summary

Both the Astoria controversy and the 1973 Fuel Crisis were situations where specific action was called for and extended delays could have had serious repercussions. Options open to decision-makers were limited because of the absence of comprehensive analysis and information. The dominant concern of decision-makers was to ameliorate the pending crisis, and although attempts were made to

acquire independent sources of data, the regulators had
to depend on information from those being regulated.
During the energy crisis of 1973, however, as environmental agencies were able to establish their own sources
of information, primarily through independent research,
and to become less reliant on the utility they were
regulating, the time factor became a less crucial variable.

> Proposition 2: Where uncertainty is high and
> time is a constraining factor, crisis
> pressures enhance the value of information
> as a resource in the competitive decision-
> making process. Available information is
> accepted because crisis prohibits further
> search.

Time pressures create a need for immediate action.
Crisis adds the threat of dire consequences if the problem
is not resolved. These pressures limit the alternatives
which can be sought. Where expediency is a factor, pre-
gathered information is particularly valuable since it
provides decision-makers with an immediate resource to
direct them toward an objective. In crisis situations,
if information is not readily available or is elsewhere
controlled, authority (as discussed in Proposition 1)
is even more severly limited.

When the information resource is inadequate, in crisis
situations the need for immediate problem resolution
increases the likelihood that decisions will involve less
risk and constitute a more conservative approach. In
the decision situations under study, government action
was called for to obtain immediate relief. Government
responsibility includes preserving its authority and
its control over a situation in a crisis. The lack of
time to consider alternative solutions to a problem
limited the degree of public debate, thereby closing off
discussion of underlying causes of the problem and
concentrating the efforts on symptomatic cures. "An
effort to avoid uncertainty may cause decisions to be made
in the context of too narrow a "system" or framework.
Moreover...there appears to be a tendency for uncertainty
to produce a bias toward over-conservatism, toward
routine ways to solve problems."[34] Established ways of
handling problems are more comfortable because they
present fewer risks. However, once such a pattern of

105

decision-making is established, the tendency may develop
to resist further attempts to enlarge the scope of the
issue. Therefore, resolution of conflict situations
may result in a form of "satisficing" or "making do".

The Astoria Controversy

Crisis heightened the effects of inadequate resources.
In the Astoria controversy, the pressures of time limited
the city's ability to find alternatives that could meet
Con Edison's demands. It was too late to search for
alternative sites to meet the utility's time schedule,
which left the Astoria expansion as the only possible
solution.

In July 1969, when Charles Luce first informed
Mayor Lindsay of the plan to construct Astoria #6 and
#7, he described an extremely serious situation if action
were not immediately taken. Luce warned that unless a
new generating facility was built, Con Edison could
not be expected to meet the electric demands of the city.
If power failures were recurrent, industry would leave
the city, with a disastrous impact upon the job market.
He noted that growing power demands required 450,000 MW
of new generating power per year. Con Edison was particularly concerned with the time factor because the lead
period for the Astoria construction, which was on an
existing facility site, was approximately 4½ years and
would be 5½ to 8 years at a new site. Moreover, Con
Edison had other problems in its system to worry about.
Construction delays at the Indian Point nuclear plant
were blamed on labor strikes and opposition from environmental groups. The purchasing of power, according to
Luce, was expensive and at best unreliable.[35] Increased
use of gas turbines was likewise expensive and often
unreliable. (They were used mostly for peak fuel consumption periods.) Moreover, Con Edison argued that
the new Queens plant would enable it to retire old and
inefficient plants, and thus reduce emissions from
them which was consistent with the clean air goals of the
1966 Memorandum. (As of 1980, no plants have been
retired.) Con Edison offered the city no other solution
for the crisis situation it presented to the city. Con
Edison promised the city a power shortage by 1974 if the
Astoria additions were not built, because no other plant
could be ready in time to meet the city's electric power
needs.

The advisory opinions received by the Mayor which supported the Astoria proposal all emphasized the immediacy of the situation and the lack of available alternatives. On September 8, 1969, the Mayor requested that the Development and Resources Corporation, chaired by David E. Lilienthal, offer recommendations on a course of action for the city. Its report on October 28, 1969, suggested "...that a new, large oil burning plant, within the City, should not be built unless there is simply no workable alternative."[36]

On December 9, 1969, the Interagency Task Force on Electric Power, under the direction of John Duba, Administrator of Municipal Services Administration, submitted its report to the Mayor. It supported the findings of the Lilienthal Report and recommended that the city take a more active role in regulating its energy supply and the development and implementation of Con Edison's construction program. It recommended approval of the Astoria proposal only reluctantly, since it could find no other suitable alternative.

Con Edison Proceeds to Build

Con Edison dramatized the situation by beginning construction of the Astoria plant while not yet having obtained the necessary permits. On December 9, 1970, Con Edison filed an application for a discharge permit from the New York State Water Resources Department (Permit 9-60-70). According to William Wall (in his City Council testimony), construction had already begun on access roads, borings, and the relocation of lines. Order "ME-6960M-Astoria Generating Station #6" included the installation of one 800 MW turbogenerator unit with steam generator equipped to fire both oil and gas. (The total estimated cost was $209,226,000, although later estimates were $100,000,000 higher). Con Edison maintained that speed was important to the completion of Astoria, and they would not wait for permits to be approved before beginning construction. "We do not believe that the provisions...apply to Astoria 6, filed just to avoid questions which might delay progress... It is our opinion that such work in any event does not require a discharge permit."[37] With certain permits lacking, Con Edison announced that excavation had begun on February 16, 1971, although according to the testimony of Wall,

107

work actually began in 1970.[38]   Aware that Con Edison
had begun construction without the necessary state
permits, DEC Commissioner Henry Diamond replied that
Con Edison was proceeding at its own risk and requested
more information from them on thermal discharge as a
basis for granting the permit.[39]   However, the state
Department of Environmental Conservation soon approved
the permit on March 25, 1971, stating that water quality
would not be contravened.

The New York City Department of Ports and Terminals
also required a permit - for the construction of foundations.
The Department asked the Army Corps of Engineers to hold
up Con Edison's application to the Corps until Ports and
Terminals issued its own permit.[40]   The permit was issued
in early April 1971.

While the permit process was pending, Con Edison
began work on the project. Con Edison reinforced the
crisis atmosphere to justify beginning construction and
perhaps influence the outcome of the regulatory process.
The construction prior to the issuance of the necessary
permits was meant to show public officials that indeed
Con Edison took its role to provide adequate electricity
for its consumers seriously. Extending the crisis
atmosphere would make it more likely that public officials
would respond favorably to Con Edison's applications,
since there was no time to search for alternatives or
consider other options.

Moreover, Con Edison forced the city to seriously
weigh the possibility of continued power failures.
The city's scarce information resources could not
counter PSC and FPC recommendations which supported
Con Edison. The city had to act quickly and approve
the plant to avoid the brown-out horrors promised by
Con Edison. The shortness of time for considering both
alternative solutions and the lead times required to
prepare other sites increased the value of information,
but there was no opportunity for the city to acquire
information that was not already available. Lack of
information and time forced the city into a competitive
bargaining situation where bargaining became a substitute
for information.

108

The 1973 Fuel Crisis

During the 1973 fuel crisis, the problem for Con Edison involved maintaining adequate fuel supplies for the generation of electricity. Since the major portion of Con Edison's residual fuel oil originated in the Middle East, the Arab embargo could have potentially affected it. If the city did not allow Con Edison to burn higher-sulfur content oil and coal, (which Con Edison claimed was available), the utility warned that the city's generating capacity would be impaired. By November 1973, the national fuel situation appeared to worsen and Con Edison filed an application for a variance to the city Air Code, necessitating a governmental response. Had the city tried to delay the application to increase its store of information, and had a power shortage then occurred, city officials would have been held responsible - and they assuredly did not want that responsibility.

The federal government gave the city no indication that the crisis would subside. President Nixon supported a temporary relaxation of environmental standards, a policy the city was trying to resist. FEO which had been handling the allocations of gasoline and home heating oil, gave no indication that it would adopt policies to reallocate residual fuel oil to utilities or to try to divert low-sulfur fuel oil to metropolitan areas where the effect of non-conforming fuel on air quality would be most harmful. If FEO had indicated that such action would be forthcoming, it would have provided guidelines to the city in establishing alternative policies for relieving the crisis.

Although EPA recommended that conservation measures be taken before variances were granted, it was not yet known whether national conservation measures would be enacted or, if they were, how effective they might be in cutting demand for electricity. Effective conservation measures could potentially cut electric power demand, but no estimates were made in PSC projections of future fuel supply needs for electric power generation. Conservation measures in the form of legislation or administrative regulations would take some time before they could be implemented and their effect made known.

The time factor forced EPA to modify its procedure for the issuance of variances. The EPA regions were advised to quickly develop a strategy for evaluating the many requests for variances that were being received. EPA hoped that it would be able to thwart, by blanket relaxation of restrictions on the sulfur content of oil, any attempt to amend the Clean Air Act of 1970. EPA also feared that if the utilities ran out of oil, the demand for coal would increase, thus straining the coal market. EPA headquarters in Washington advised the regions that the time between public notice of hearings and hearing dates could be reduced. The effect of this on local environmental agencies was to generate immediate action. However, EPA warned that oil companies needed lead time to obtain fuel, and headquarters needed time to evaluate the applications. Because EPA was soon overwhelmed with applications for variances, the regions were asked to give preliminary analyses justifying the need of a variance in each state by November 9, 1973. EPA said it would supply the regions with technical support for discussions with the suppliers in addition to air quality analyses. These procedures were to be temporary for the period of the projected winter's fuel crisis. The Con Edison variance application procedure was acted upon within this framework. EPA notified DEC that hearings could be held on 10 days notice instead of the required 30 days in view of the PSC certification of insufficiency already obtained by Con Edison. EPA stated that any variance issued by a state was considered a revision of the State Implementation Plan and was subject to EPA approval. (Otherwise it would not be subject to enforcement and the states would be subject to citizen suits.) EPA stressed that all other reasonable measures must be taken before any variance could be granted on the basis of need. EPA Deputy Regional Administrator Eric Outwater reluctantly told Deputy DEC Commissioner James Biggane that he would approve a public notice period of 10 days if he were assured that adequate publicity would be given.[41] The local environmental agencies, with severe time constraints operating, seemed to possess little discretion other than to determine by exactly how much, environmental standards would be relaxed.

The failure of the national and state governments to offer guidance or hard information on the fuel situation reinforced the crisis pressures that were limiting the

options available to city officials. Data could not
be put together fast enough to make a substantial case
supporting the maintenance of environmental standards.
The sense of panic left little time for careful analysis
of the data that was available, let alone for a search
for additional sources.

Crisis Limits Options

After the city made its decision on November 19th,
(prohibiting coal), Con Edison Chairman Luce said CEPA
was "playing Russian roulette with its electric power
supply."[42] Con Edison announced it was going ahead with
its coal conversion program even before the state issued
its ruling.[43] Con Edison Vice-President Bertram Schwartz
explained that it was necessary to stockpile coal
immediately because of market instability. Con Edison
hoped the state would rule favorably, making it possible
to appeal the city's objections before a special panel
or the courts.[44] To emphasize its position, Con Edison
informed PSC that, if their application for coal was
rejected, the utility was prepared to cut heat on subways
and blackout selected areas of the city.[45] Con Edison,
thus perpetuated the crisis atmosphere by announcing it
would begin purchasing coal without government approval
(and perhaps pressuring the government to grant permission)
and threatening a worse crisis if their demands were not
met.

In December 1973, the price of oil rose to $18.50
per barrel. Musicus, now head of the Emergency Energy
Supply Task Force, hinted that he might ask PSC for a
statewide 5% voltage reduction.[46] Con Edison quickly
replied that a voltage reduction would be unnecessary if
it were permitted to burn coal.[47]

Con Edison Vice-President Harry Woodbury wrote to
CEPA Administrator Herbert Elish, asking him to reconsider
the November variance and to permit the use of coal.[48]
The New England Petroleum Corporation (NEPCO), had informed
Con Edison that it was reducing its delivery by 600,000
barrels in December, and part of its shipment would be
1% sulfur oil. The second major supplier, Hess, had
likewise informed Con Edison that its delivery would be
1.25% sulfur oil. Con Edison Vice-President Woodbury
was worried that, because of the outage at Indian Point #2,

111

which would probably last until sometime in January, the
situation was more severe than had been earlier anticipated. He argued that using coal would not increase
SO_2 concentration in the air any more than the use of
non-conforming oil, and particulates would be increased
only at points of emission.

Because information on available fuel supplies was
unreliable, no environmental agency could effectively
challenge Con Edison or other regulatory agencies on that
issue. Because the situation demanded immediate attention,
officials were compelled to either stabilize the situation
or suffer the wrath of the public if the worst case
situation suggested by Con Edison ever materialized.

> Proposition 3: The absence of advance planning,
> scanning, and analysis, and goal or priority
> formation on the part of any of the actors
> limits the options perceived by them and
> weakens their commitment to seek a particular
> outcome. The greater the prior analysis and
> goal identification of an actor, the greater
> their influence on decision outcomes, other
> things being equal.

Advance planning and information gathering mechanisms
are political resources. As in Proposition 1, where
information controlled by clients limited the authority
of the government agency, the absence of preformed goals
also limits options because decision-makers are unprepared
to cope with the situation and have no focused goals,
values, priorities, or assumptions. Bargains will be
accepted by the government agency only after formal negotiations
to resolve value conflicts among private actors has occurred,
thus minimizing comprehensive analysis.[9] In situations
where private actors can threaten to take reprisals,
interference with agency integrity can occur as pressure
increases to reach a compromised solution.

The absence of prior planning by an agency may limit
general public involvement and interest. The lack of
routine mechanisms for securing input from the public
and other government agencies limits both the amount of
new information generated and issue awareness.

Inadequate information, crisis pressures, and the
absence of preformed planning (Propositions 1, 2, and 3)
combine to restrict options open to decision-makers in
a competitive bargaining situation. The existence of
each of these factors cuts into the authority of an
agency affecting the range of outcomes of decision
situations.

The Astoria Controversy

In this decision situation the greater experience
of the private sphere in preformed activity was a
significant political resource. The planning function
for providing adequate electric power generation was
performed by Con Edison without either consultation
with the city or its electric customers.

Although Con Edison submitted a Ten Year Program
to the Mayor in 1966 and a revised Ten Year Program in
1969, the city not only lacked the jurisdiction to
review it, but did not have staff qualified to evaluate
it. Con Edison's revised Ten Year Program was submitted
as an addendum to the original proposal for the Astoria
#6 and #7 plants. Con Edison stated that the revisions
were due to delays in the installation of new equipment
and to upward projections of electric growth rates.
The program included current available capacity, sources
of additional power (e.g., new plants, gas turbines),
planned purchases through 1972, and proposed retirements.

Con Edison subsequently made public a Twenty Year
Plan in 1972 and a Twenty Year Advance Plan in 1973,
fulfilling requirements of the 1972 New York State
Public Service Law* which required annual reports on
long-range plans. The law required utilities to demonstrate how the forecasted growth rate would be met while
satisfying environmental and economic goals. Con Edison's
plan was similar to its 1969 program in that it listed

---

*Public Service Law, New York State, Section 149-b, "The
members of the New York power pool shall prepare and
submit annually to the department...a single comprehensive
long-range plan for future operations drawn pursuant to
regulations issued by the commission."

new facilities to be constructed, facilities to be retired, and expected purchases of power. A new feature was the inclusion of funds to be committed to research and development programs of the Electric Power Research Institute. Con Edison forecasts were based on growth projections of the various users in the city and the economic conditions of the service area.

Con Edison's thoroughness in planning to meet its primary objective of satisfying electric power demand appears in stark contrast to the activity of the city, devoid of dependable statistics and analysis. The city, lacking ongoing regulatory and oversight functions, commanded no substantive policy or objectives with which to evaluate Con Edison plans.

The 1973 Fuel Crisis

Con Edison's long-term strategy was to resist regulations limiting the sulfur content of the fuel it used and to obtain permission to burn coal. During the period September 1973 through March 1974, Con Edison's oil suppliers did not meet delivery schedules, did not provide required volumes of conforming oil, and did increase prices. Con Edison exaggerated the long-term impact of these facts and put them to use to alter long-term environmental regulatory policies.

In attempting to force CEPA to allow Con Edison to burn coal at some of its plants, the company explained that if the environmental agencies waited too long to grant approval, the need for coal would be substantially increased since adequate lead time is necessary to procure coal.[50] Con Edison pressured CEPA into approving coal by saying that once EPA had granted approval, Con Edison would be at a disadvantage in its efforts to obtain coal if CEPA required more time to deliberate. The arguments in favor of coal were essentially: (1) insufficient time existed to obtain the necessary oil; (2) there was limited knowledge of the availability of fuel supplies; and (3) the absence of any response from FEO on Con Edison's requests for additional oil - to compensate for oil which would have been saved had Ravenswood gone to coal - necessitated the use of coal at Ravenswood immediately.[51] However, the city could not counter these arguments since

114

it had few alternatives to offer Con Edison having not
provided for fuel shortage contingencies.

Of course, some individuals felt that the entire
East Coast oil shortage was being manipulated by the
oil monopolies to create scarcity during a period when
Con Edison's profits were up 20%.[52] It was suggested
that oil and coal companies would use the crisis to
obtain objectives they had been seeking in the past,
that is, the relaxation of air quality standards and,
by dramatizing short-run crises, the maintenance of
high long-term demand until demand could be filled by
new and more profitable nuclear plants.[53]

When the Arab embargo began in the fall of 1973,
Con Edison was well-prepared with arguments to support
the position of increased purchasing freedom in the
fuel market. Con Edison had available estimates of
plant capacity, fuel reserves, and anticipated supplies
of conforming fuel. In order to generate public support
for its position, Con Edison calculated the cost-savings
of millions of dollars to the consumer if high-sulfur
fuel were allowed.[54]

The city, on the other hand, had no comparable
experience with such statistics with which to challenge
Con Edison's presentation. Other than the Municipal
Services Administration's involvement with problems of
local fuel supply and delivery, the city had no prior
need to analyze fuel supply data, or even to prepare
plans to assist Con Edison in meeting its fuel supply
requirements.

One alternative that was stressed at all levels of
government was the use of conservation measures to reduce
the demand for fuel. However, as discussed earlier,
there were no reliable estimates which the city (or
any other level of government) had at its disposal
to determine the amount of energy savings that conservation measures would represent.

Summary

The paucity of government activity in fuel supply
problems and utility regulation in general enabled Con
Edison to assume the function of determining the energy

requirements for its own service area as well as how
it would meet them. The city, forced to define the
problems solely as a supply-crisis situation, accepted
bargaining as the strategy. On the short term, the
city made concessions to Con Edison because their options
were limited even before the bargaining had begun.

By the time of the 1973 fuel crisis, no substantial
planning had been done by the city toward developing
either an energy policy or procedures which would minimize
pollution effects in the event of a fuel shortage. The
city had never monitored Con Edison's oil supply system
and had no knowledge of Con Edison's fuel needs or sources
of supply. Con Edison's crisis perspective left the city
insufficient time to gather its own information and
develop contingency plans to cope with the kind of
emergency situation which was facing the city. The absence
of this kind of preformed activity by the public sector
reinforced the strength of Con Edison's analysis of the
crisis situation in the political sphere.

> Proposition 4: When policy objectives of
> governmental actors are uncertain or in
> conflict, the impact of positive government
> action is diminished.

Administrative authorities are pressured to maximize
organizational objectives which help shape policy decisions.
One of the responsibilities of environmental agencies is
to act as a watchdog to insure that actions taken in both
the public and private sectors do not cause environmental
deterioration. Utility regulatory and advisory agencies
are concerned with providing reliable electric power at
levels demanded by users. Where power plant siting is
at issue, these two sets of objectives come into conflict;
the power agency is less concerned about the environmental impact of the new plant than its ability to provide
electricity. From the environmentalist's perspective,
any negative impact should be minimized, requiring either
a change of site or additional expenditures for pollution
control equipment.

For city government as a whole, the choice or the
tradeoff between the two objectives was never resolved.
When goals of actors are well-defined, strategy designed
to meet objectives can be more precisely formulated.

116

However, when multiple and ambiguous goals predominate, the path of action is less clear. Action is taken then in response to external stimuli while actors try to satisfy more than one goal simultaneously.

Wildavsky comments: "The larger the number of objectives...the greater the number of interests they encompass."[55] These potentially conflicting objectives are best resolved in the political arena.[56] However, when goals of actors are in conflict and resources are unevenly distributed, the outcome in the political arena may be skewed before bargaining occurs. Moreover, competitive values held at different levels of authority may lead to conflicting policies, which in turn may hamper the development of coordinated activity and planning.

The Astoria Controversy

In the Astoria controversy, city officials were faced with a dilemma defined as a conflict between power and pollution. If the city approved the two new Astoria plants, it ran the risk of violating air quality standards and jeopardizing the health and safety of its citizens. The areas of the city which would be most affected by emissions from the Astoria plant were those areas which did not yet meet federal air quality standards. According to federal environmental officials, these areas would be unable to do so with the addition of increased emissions from the Astoria plant. If the city prohibited Con Edison from building the plants, subsequent power failures could impair the safety of New Yorkers with severe political repercussions; the onus would be on city officials. Both brown-outs and air pollution alerts during the summer of 1970, dramatized the seriousness of the situation.

Each administrative level of government was subject to different pressures, different constituents, and different procedures for carrying out their mandates. These variables helped shape agency values and policies. There was sharp variation in these external factors across hierarchical levels as well as within any given government jurisdiction. Due to fiscal pressures, New York City was particularly susceptible to pressure by local industry and real estate groups. Their view was represented by Kenneth Patton of the Economic Development Administration, a member of ICPU, who argued that the city was dependent

on industry for its tax base, and that higher electric
costs and poor service encouraged resettlement outside
the city, with reduced city revenues as a result. He
also warned that power shortages would hamper the city's
goal of creating 3,000 new jobs.[57]   For business and
industry, if there were a choice between power and clean
air, the former would be preferred.

Groups such as the Central Labor Council of the
AFL-CIO, New York Chamber of Commerce, Association for
a Better New York and the Real Estate Board of New York,
Inc., also expressed concern with maintaining a healthy
economic environment and preventing power shortages due
to inadequate generating capacity.   Real estate and
construction industry representatives argued that new
office space required increased power for air conditioners,
elevators, lighting and office equipment.   Moreover,
benefits from the new Astoria plant would include additional
real estate tax revenues and the creation of new jobs.

Commitments to positive action by government officials
were hampered by a lack of clear objectives within the
public domain.   Political variables tended to predominate
as some local legislators sought to oppose Con Edison
with action in the city legislature.   Most legislators were
moved more by political loyalties than the need for concerted
action.

On the local level, the Mayor sought a compromise
which limited the Astoria expansion to one plant.   However,
the City Council (a legislative body) was the site for
continued opposition.   Councilmembers are more responsive
to strongly voiced concerns of their constituents as
opposed to the broad based constituency of the Mayor.
The Mayor's operant environment, i.e., pressures,
constituents and methods of operation differed from the
Council which extended the life of the issue.

The Manton Bill

The first major effort to halt the Astoria plant
expansion was initiated by Councilman Thomas Manton,
representing the communities of Astoria, Long Island City,
Woodside, Maspeth, and Sunnyside.   Con Edison and air
pollution were popular issues in the community, and
Manton took this into account.   On October 14, 1970, he

introduced a bill into the City Council prohibiting the
use of new fossil-fuel burning generators of over twenty
MW capacity. The penalties were to be $1,000 and/or one
year imprisonment. "This local law shall not apply to the
operation of any fossil fuel burning electric generator
capable of generating twenty MW or more of electric power,
which had been in active operation within the City as of
October 1, 1970."[56] The Manton bill was, of course, an
attempt to ban the construction of any new power plants
in the city. Manton argued with critics of the bill who
asked why other communities should receive New York's
pollution from electric power generation. He replied that
people who resided in suburbia and worked in New York
City benefited from the quality of life in the city.
Their property value was enhanced because of the
accessibility to the cultural, vocational, and financial
attributes of the city. Two million lives in Queens
would be affected by the plant, while an upstate plant
would affect fewer people, and affect them less severely.

The bill could not be forced out of the Environmental
Protection Committee of the Council for a vote on the
Council floor, and was never voted upon. Manton had
counted 19 potential votes in favor of the bill - a
passing vote - but he needed 25 votes if the Mayor vetoed
it. If passed, the bill would have been a slap in the
Mayor's face, since he had already approved construction
of Astoria #6 - an 800 MW facility. The Mayor rarely
vetoes Council bills because he does not want to antagonize
a segment of his constituency, and he usually does not
have to use veto power because of his special influence
within the Council. The Majority Leader of the Council
and the Mayor have a cooperative relationship, the former
dealing directly with the Mayor on Council matters.
The Mayor therefore has direct input into Council
activities through the Majority Leader, who controls
patronage for Councilpersons, influences the appointment
of committee chairpersons, and controls the movement of
bills from committee to the Council floor.

Manton explained that the failure of the Council
to take action on his bill was due to a lack of support
from councilmembers with constituencies not directly
affected by the pollution from the Astoria plant, and
who were more sensitive to industry and Con Edison views,
i.e., that a power shortage was the overriding danger.

Another influential Councilman, Donald Manes of Queens, was absent from the Committee vote after he promised support. Matthew Troy of Queens, who was not shy about taking on the Mayor on other issues, gave only lip service to Manton's efforts. The Manton bill represented an attack on both Council leadership and the Mayor. The fact that the Manton bill did not get to the floor for a vote, although Manton personally counted enough votes for success, indicated both substantial opposition and noninterest. Manton could only count on support from councilmembers whose districts were directly involved and a few liberals who supported environmental interests at the time of reckoning. The Majority Leader, with all his political influence, had no need to apply pressure because he had no constituent interests to satisfy on this matter and therefore could safely oppose the bill. He also had no need to jeopardize his own relationship with the Mayor.

Army Corps of Engineers Hearings

The interaction of federal agencies continued through 1972. While NAPCA counseled CEPA of the adverse conditions which would result from the Astoria expansion even with the use of low-sulfur content fuel, the result of federal Army Corps of Engineers hearings in March 1972 did not provide environmentalists with an opportunity to rejoice. Under pressure from environmentalists, the Army Corps of Engineers invoked the provisions of the National Environmental Quality Act of 1969, delaying for thirty days the issuance of any construction permit until an environmental impact statement was received. The Astoria plant required the dredging and building of inflow and outflow pipes, and it is in the jurisdiction of the Corps to approve any construction on navigable waters. The Department of Interior's Bureau of Fish and Wildlife asked for an environmental statement and more time for reviews,[59] as did the Water Quality Office of the federal EPA.[60] The hearings took two days and gave the community an opportunity to voice its opinion, which had little effect on events. The testimony was evaluated by the Corps, which concluded that it now had a basis for the issuance of construction and discharge permits to Con Edison.

Conflicting Objectives in Retrospect

Fulfillment of policy objectives on one level of
government may be stymied because of conflicting policy
objectives on a higher level of government. CEPA argued
for a comprehensive policy toward power plant siting
because it was concerned with the environmental impact
of unlimited and unplanned electric demand. The city's
Economic Development Administration's policy of unlimited
office space construction conflicted with CEPA's thrust
for energy conservation. When CEPA tried to expand the
issue to examine the implications of continued electric
growth, it was hampered by the state PSC policy of supporting
continued electric growth.[61] PSC had had more independence
to protect the interests of its constituents, the utilities,
than had the newer DEC.

The PSC approved of the Astoria plant based both on
power and environmental arguments. Harold Colbeth, Jr.,
Acting Director of the PSC Electric Division, claimed that
the two new plants would release less sulfur oxides than
the existing older plants. However, he also claimed that
any contribution by the Astoria expansion would represent
only a small addition of .01 ppm.[62] In addition, he
maintained, the production of electricity was necessary
to raise and maintain the standard of living, especially of
the poor. PSC policy had encouraged electric heating, the
building of plants close to urban centers, and the construction of larger units (whose outages would have a greater
effect on the system).[63] PSC policies, such as the inclusion
of promotional advertising in computing the rate base
while omitting the environmental costs of electric power
generation, made it difficult for a local environmental
agency and DEC to authoritatively develop a policy toward
protecting the environment. CEPA received little support
from DEC, which quickly approved the Astoria expansion
and effectively removed any state objection based on
environmental effects. With each environmental agency
producing different analyses of environmental impact,
no authoritative assessment existed. This disparity
over the effects on air and water quality made it
extremely difficult for newly formed environmental agencies
to force power or energy agencies to include environmental
considerations when power plant siting decisions were
made. The failure to resolve conflicts among different
value systems among hierarchical levels moved the
problem in the political arena. The actor who could

121

clearly define his objective - and demonstrate the
potentiality of greater risk to the public if such
goals were not met - had a sizeable advantage. The
problem of adequate electric supply was addressed in
a limited form, and only when external events forced
the problem to appear as a crisis. Such a crisis
occurred again in 1973.

The 1973 Fuel Crisis

By 1973, CEPA had tightened air quality regulations
and reduced the amount of sulfur allowed in fuel oil.
However, Con Edison still presented a problem for CEPA.
In 1970, after Con Edison had been granted a variance
to burn coal at Arthur Kill only if necessary, it was
discovered that Con Edison had violated the variance by
working the plant at capacity. PSC restrained CEPA from
filing a court suit, insisting the city did not have the
authority to regulate power. The conflict between the
environmental values of CEPA and the power concerns
of PSC continued into the fall of 1973. PSC refused to
lower its reserve requirements for utilities and immediately
granted Con Edison a certificate of fuel insufficiency.
CEPA's options were only to decide what level of sulfur
should be permitted and whether coal should be allowed
as an alternative to oil. CEPA wanted a fuller investigation of the situation, but pressure by PSC forced DEC
to grant Con Edison its variance. PSC continued to
denounce CEPA and EPA for not allowing coal at Arthur Kill
#3 and Ravenswood #3.[64]

CEPA, in trying to formulate a course of action for
the city had to establish what fuel oil would be available
to Con Edison before it would feel compelled to allow
the burning of coal. The city contacted William Simon
at FEO urging a quick decision as to whether mandatory
allocation of residual oil would be made to Con Edison.
The city believed that unless mandatory allocations could
be made, there would be a shortfall even if the city
allowed coal.[65] Since FEO had failed to respond with
mandatory allocations of low-sulfur fuel oil, CEPA had to
act on the DEC exception to the SIP before it knew in
actuality what the fuel situation would be. Although EPA
was asked by FEO to designate areas which should receive
low-sulfur fuel, until a mandatory allocation program was
underway, there could be no effect on current allocations
of fuel, and CEPA planning was therefore hampered.[66] CEPA

122

amended its November 19th decision on December 18, 1973 to allow Con Edison to purchase and store coal not exceeding 300,000 tons. The decision was based on the EPA decision of December 13, 1973 to allow coal at Arthur Kill #30 and the agreement between FEO and EPA to allow certain utilities to switch to coal. A deal was made to permit coal at Arthur Kill if the Sewarren plant in New Jersey ceased burning coal. (Arthur Kill #30 was considered cleaner, and its emissions would have less impact on air quality in the area than would the New Jersey plant.) As a result, the city had little choice but to conform to this agreement lacking assurances that emergency supplies of oil would be forthcoming. CEPA's original position of prohibiting the burning of coal in New York City because of its extreme effect on air quality was weakened because of uncertainty and conflict on other levels of government. A disappointed CEPA administrator Herb Elish hoped more stringent power conservation measures would now be considered.[67]

EPA

The policy of EPA - that any conversions to coal be limited in number and be short-term in nature - turned out to conflict with FEO encouragement of coal conversion by any utility that had the capability to convert.[68] This confusion left the city with little idea of which set of objectives the national government supported.

EPA supported the city, stating that economic savings should not be considered as a factor in promoting conversion to coal. "The EPA must show that it is aware of the cheaper coal cost factor, and attempt to prove that such costs are usually less onerous than the utilities argue...in the interests of public health."[69] However, this policy put EPA into direct conflict with both FEO and local power authorities.

At times EPA also appeared at odds with the White House, which advocated legislation to relax air quality regulations, because the high cost of low-sulfur fuel was inflationary. Russell Train said he would oppose the President on such measures as designating tall stacks as a pollution control device and eliminating the non-deterioration clause of the Clean Air Act. "Energy problems are providing an opportunity for people to attack the environmental movement."[70] FEO seemed to have more influence with the President; Train reported he had seen

123

very little of the President since he had taken office, while the FEO director saw him twice a week.[71]

The policy conflicts among these agencies made it difficult for any uniform direction to emerge. The lack of any coordinating mechanism instead encouraged the domination of political variables, i.e., by actors with the greatest resources.

Agreement of Goals

When agencies were in agreement over objectives, it was reflected in policy statements and definitive action. Neither CEPA nor EPA were anxious for Con Edison to extend coal burning to the Ravenswood plant. Since there was a limited storage capacity at Ravenswood, contracting for coal would more likely lead to its use. CEPA did not believe it would be necessary to use coal at all after March 31, 1974, since the oil supply situation had improved.[72] EPA felt that approval of coal for Ravenswood would contravene the EPA-FEO program of converting only those plants to coal which would produce the least health hazards, although EPA assured Con Edison that all its requests for additional supplies of residual oil would be forwarded to FEO.[73] "It is not our intention to plunge precipitously into the conversion of oil-burning equipment to coal use when the affected facility potentially impacts an area which exceeds primary ambient air quality standards."[74] Thus any attempts to extend coal burning to other Con Edison plants met with strong disfavor by environmental agencies.

Interactive Aspects

CEPA itself had multiple objectives. The Emergency Energy Supply Task Force was responsible to CEPA Administrator Robert Low. The Task Force dealt primarily with the fuel shortage, but it had to consider the environmental repercussions of its actions. On one hand, it was required to ensure that the city had adequate energy, and on the other that air quality would not deteriorate. Moreover, the departments of Purchase, Rent and Housing, Consumer Affairs and Corporation Counsel, all handled some aspects of the fuel crisis problem. A department with separate goals could potentially pursue a path satisfactory to its specific set of goals but in direct conflict with another department's.

124

Summary

Much of the actual decision-making was done on the local level. Local governments are especially vulnerable to business and real estate lobbies, particularly in New York. Since national guidelines were absent, numerous agencies on a hierarchical scale had a role in the resolution of conflicts, a situation that brought to the surface underlying conflict between energy and environmental agencies in the form of conflicting goals. "All multiplicity of decision-centers, in the form of either independent governmental units or subsystems within large organizations, exercise a degree of legal or de facto autonomy in pursuing goals which may or may not relate to comprehensive environmental planning."[75] When an issue is characterized by numerous decision-making centers pursuing conflicting goals, perceptions of risk, clarity and strength of goals become important factors in determining outcomes.

> Proposition 5: Where the characteristics
> of decision-making situations discourage
> definitive action and evaluation of hard
> data, they tend to emphasize the dis-
> semination of symbols.

Symbolic action fosters satisfaction and reassurance to those to whom it is directed. Symbolic acts may be aimed at the public, interest groups, or private factions to assure them they are being understood. Symbolic actions attempt to placate a constituency. Crisis situations are particularly susceptible to symbolic actions because of the time constraints that make substantive policy changes problematic.

Language justifying actions may give the impression that the public interest is being protected. Where public knowledge is at a low level of understanding, there is a greater tendency toward symbolic and reassuring language.[76] "The most obvious kind of dissemination of symbolic satisfaction is to be found in administrative dicta accompanying decisions and orders, in press releases..."[77] When the "real" issue is not on the agenda because it is precluded by crisis situation considerations, symbolic action may substitute. Murray Edelman suggests that statutes may be symbolic by containing "strong assurances that the public or public interest will be protected" and states that "the most widely-publicized regulatory provisions always include

125

other operational standards connoting fairness, balance
or equity."78

The Astoria Controversy

On a hot summer's Saturday, August 22, 1970, the Mayor
announced his decision. His "Solomon-like" response
reflected his reluctance to challenge the private sector
(Con Edison and its supporters) perhaps because of his
forthcoming Presidential bid which might require their
campaign contributions. More likely, he did not want to
be blamed for the occurence of a power shortage if he
refused Con Edison permission to build additional facilities.
In his statement, he remarked that disagreement had existed
on every level of government. Federal and state power
agencies supported the Astoria facility while agencies
concerned with the environment were opposed. The Mayor
commented that there were uncontrolled national and international forces competing with the city, which had the
least resources and authority to deal with the situation.
He noted that power agencies explained it was unlikely that
the Astoria installation could be fueled by natural gas,
but that since FPC had approved of the proposal, and they
controlled natural gas, "...this represented a decision as
much as an opinion."79 Further, he suggested that pollution
might be reduced from other sources, automobiles, for
instance. This would reduce the danger point of emissions
from the Astoria plant. The Mayor felt that the construction
of an 800 MW plant, or one half the requested plant was
consistent with the 1966 Memorandum of Understanding with
Con Edison. It was decided that Con Edison would: (1) try
to use natural gas or low-sulfur content fuels; (2) eliminate
the use of coal-fueled plants by October 1971; (3) invest
$4 million in the research and development of anti-pollution
techniques; and (4) convert the rest of the system to low-
pollutant fuels. Besides the Astoria plant, by 1974 Con
Edison would have 300 MW built outside the city. It was
hoped that this capacity would meet the city's needs. The
city also agreed to rent the use of transmission lines which
would be built along the city-owned Croton acqueduct. This
would increase Con Edison's ability to purchase power from
the north.

The Agreement with Con Edison also expressed the need
for a national energy policy. "The failure of national
policy and national leadership in recent years has left

us no alternatives with regard to the expansion of the
Astoria plant - and in fact, with regard to the area of
power generation in general, the Federal government has
been sadly lacking...the policies of the FPC, in combination
with those of the Department of Interior, deny us the fuel
that would make it possible to eliminate almost completely
sulfur dioxide and particulate emissions, and make nitrous
oxides controllable... What stands in the way of both an
adequate supply of power and cleaner air for New York and
every city is not some technological obstacle, but the
decisions that men make."[80]

The Memorandum of Understanding of August 22, 1970,
(between the city and Con Edison), created the illusion
that differences were being reconciled; however, misleading
statements and promises concealed the conflict that still
existed. In 1970, CEPA could expect support from interest
groups by using symbolic language which justified its
decision. The Memorandum was a conciliatory exercise
containing language aimed at satisfying environmentalists
as well as those supporting Con Edison. The following
examples are illustrative.

(1) Oftentimes public decision-makers will say they
will act on an issue when they know constraining factors
will prevent the action from occurring. This is the
symbolic aspect of a compromise or agreement which is
placed there to offset the concessions that have been made.
In order to reassure the general public that the city and
Con Edison considered environmental protection a foremost
priority, it was agreed that Con Edison would make every
reasonable effort to obtain natural gas for the Astoria
plant (natural gas being preferable to oil or coal because,
although emissions of nitrogen oxides remain constant,
sulfur emissions are negligible). However, this new
Memorandum between Con Edison and the city contained some
inherent contradictions. In one paragraph FPC and PSC
advised the city that a new plant using natural gas
exclusively was unrealistic, given the current shortages.
In a later paragraph the Mayor explained that his decision
to reduce the plant size at Astoria from 1,600 MW to 800 MW
was based on the "...failure of the FPC to allocate natural
gas in sufficient quantities to power a 1,600 MW expansion."
This section of the Memorandum of Understanding reflected
the pessimism concerning the use of natural gas. Luce had
said he was prepared to use natural gas, but "at the present

time natural gas is not available in the required volumes."[81]
In a subsequent statement he said he could not build the
Astoria plants if they depended on natural gas.[82] FPC
advised the Mayor that no new quantities of natural gas
would be made available for Astoria.[83] PSC concurred with
this view, stating: "From what we know of the natural gas
situation, it would not be realistic to expect that the
Astoria units could be fueled by natural gas..."[84] When
the city went directly to the federal government, the
situation was further confirmed. CEPA Administrator Kretchmer
met with Secretary of the Interior Walter Hickle to clarify
the natural gas situation and he was told that Con Edison
could only expect a quantity amounting to one-eighth of its
1969 consumption.[85]

     Nevertheless, these opinions were interpreted in the
Memorandum to mean that if FPC, which controls natural gas
allocation, approved the Astoria plant expansion, then a
decision to make natural gas available was implied. "Since
the FPC also controls the allocation of natural gas through-
out the country, this represents a decision as much as an
opinion."[86] This logic was the basis for including natural
gas as a condition for approval by the city of the Astoria
expansion, effectively ignoring the possibility that FPC
might have approved of the plants without any commitment
to providing natural gas. In essence, the Memorandum said
it was unlikely that natural gas would be available, but
Con Edison must make every effort to obtain it. The reliance
upon natural gas and its inclusion in the Memorandum was
an attempt to make the city's decision more palatable to
the broader public, especially environmental interests.
The promulgation of conditions which all parties knew could
not be met was a strategy in which no participant could
lose. No one could be held responsible if the conditions
were not met. It was a symbolic gesture lacking any substance or measure of reality.

     (2) Another example of symbolism designed to make the
Agreement more palatable to all parties involved the actual
shutting down of power plants. The 1970 Memorandum contained
a provision stating that if the city found the Air Code
being violated, it would close the plant involved. This
was based on a recommendation of ICPU in its majority
report to the Mayor. Realistically, it would have been
extremely difficult to close an operational plant which
provided baseload power without incurring opposition from
a public which feared brown-outs and blackouts. Moreover,

there most likely would be opposition from utility regulatory agencies, and Con Edison and its investors, to any proposal which would close a plant that cost over $300 million. (In fact, Con Edison argued before the Army Corps of Engineers that it had already committed $120 million and spent $30 million with the assumption that it would get the necessary government approval.[87] The utility apparently attributed so much weight to the argument that it actually began construction before the necessary state permits were issued.) This plant closing condition of the Memorandum was another attempt by the city to make it appear no environmental damage would be done, although EPA definitely said that any additions to the Astoria complex, even with lower sulfur fuel, would prevent certain areas of the city from meeting federal air quality standards. It was a symbolic move by the city to demonstrate that regulatory functions were being exercised.

(3) Vague language in agreements which later generate loopholes or oversights may be the result of an attempt to keep something controversial off the agenda. Such acts are symbolic since they are geared toward eliciting public support while realities are masked or ignored. The 1970 Memorandum contained an omission which some city officials later said was a result of ignorance, but which a Con Edison representative said was an intentional omission involving the tacit understanding of the Mayor.[88] The subject was the use of gas turbines, which use expensive distillate oil, pollute more heavily, use 5% more fuel per megawatt output, but have the advantages of being more quickly constructed and being mounted on barges near steam generating sites.[89] In the past Con Edison had employed gas turbines to meet peak needs without supervision by the DAR. Since gas turbines technically are not boilers, the city did not consider their use to be in violation of the 1966 Memorandum, which prohibited the building of new fossil-fuel plants in the metropolitan area. According to city officials, Con Edison had informed the city neither of the extent to which gas turbines were being employed nor their level of emissions. Subsequent spot checks by DAR revealed that in some cases they were being used for base-load generation. DAR also discovered that there were 15 MW of gas turbines operating at Astoria.[90] The omission of gas turbine regulations in the 1970 Memorandum was a loophole which Con Edison could use to fill in gaps

in its system without stringent regulation. If the
omission occurred with knowledge of the City Hall aides
who drew up the Memorandum, it may have been part of a
bargain made with Con Edison in exchange for reducing
the Astoria plants by half. Gas turbines could make up
for a small part of the missing 800 MW which were denied
Con Edison. Nevertheless, the gas turbine situation was
an example of the city having been unable to take substantive
action and therefore having ignored the issue.

Identification with the Public Interest

        Symbolic action may be seen when appeals are made to
the public interest. Referring to vague values which are
widely accepted invokes positive responses, although their
meaning may not be clear. The values do not have to be
explained because of the natural emotional response forthcoming. For example, everyone wants to protect the environment, but definitions of what that means to each community
or individual differ and require specific programmatic
analysis, which may actually promote controversy. Ambiguity
of language facilitates agreement and flexibility to bargain.

        Proponents of the Astoria expansion tried to legitimize
their position by demonstrating their concern for the public
interest and symbolic appeal to accepted public goals. It
was contended that Astoria #6 and #7 were needed to meet
base-load requirements.[91] According to Con Edison, part
of the need was due to environmental demands requiring
increased electric power (i.e., environmental waste treat-
ment abatement facilities,[92] mass transit and air conditioners).[93] Additional power was also needed to create new
jobs resulting from construction of new office space, the
Second Avenue subway, and additional fire and police
stations.[94] The creation of these jobs was suggested as a
means to generate income for the city. A class-struggle
argument was even raised, implying that power was needed
to service appliances that the poor were struggling to
aspire to, and which the middle class already owned. To
meet all these needs, Con Edison estimated that it needed
450 MW of new generating power each year.[95] Thus Con
Edison's needs for additional power plants were justified
to meet public demand for increased service. However,
according to CEPA, the problem of adequate power was not
one of base-load capacity but one of meeting peak demand,
which could be seen from the increases needed in reserve

capacity during the summer months. Con Edison also claimed that without Astoria #6 and #7, the power shortages resulting would encourage industrial abandonment of the city. The validity of these assertions could not be challenged in the available time. Alternative explanations therefore had to be overlooked (e.g., increased taxes, expensive labor market, and the quality of life).

Since clean air was the issue at hand, Con Edison appealed to environmental values. Con Edison attempted to demonstrate that the air would be cleaner with the Astoria additions by showing how effectively emissions had been reduced, from 1966 to 1971, predating emission control laws.[96] Con Edison predicted that when Astoria was converted to low-sulfur fuel, with the additions, total sulfur dioxide emissions would be 76% less in 1966.[97] These statistics do not, however, indicate whether federal air quality standards will be met.

While Con Edison publicly supported reduced emissions, it privately opposed laws or regulations which reduced the sulfur content of fuel, even though the reason emissions had already been reduced was the use of cleaner fuel. Luce publicly stated that the use of low-sulfur oil would be compatible with environmental goals.[98] Con Edison was optimistic that they could obtain low-sulfur oil. "Today we are confident that we can obtain enough .37% sulfur fuel for the new capacity, and probably for the entire plant..."[99] Con Edison said it would use the .37% sulfur oil at Astoria by the spring of 1972.[100] However, the proposed Air Code required .3% sulfur oil after October 1972 anyway. Use of .37% sulfur oil at Astoria in return for permission to expand was therefore a symbolic statement and a misleading benefit.[101] Nevertheless, at subsequent hearings on the proposed new Air Code, Luce testified that low-sulfur fuel would increase fuel costs, which would eventually increase taxes, rents, and electric bills.[102] Luce also said that if low-sulfur oil were cheap enough, Con Edison could convert all existing boilers.[103] (However, the lower the sulfur content in oil, the higher the cost of the fuel becomes.) Luce suggested that October 1, 1971, was too soon for Con Edison to obtain .3% fuel, which would not make that much of a difference.[104] Oil companies agreed with Con Edison that the cost was too high and adequate supplies could not be guaranteed.[105] However, a reduction from .37% to .3% represented a 20% reduction in sulfur emissions,[106] which would have been substantial. Eventually, the Air

131

Code was revised when Local Law 49 was passed, and Con Edison received a one-year extension allowing it to burn fuel with a sulfur content averaging .55%. Despite public statements supporting the use of low-sulfur fuel, Con Edison was able to postpone the requirements.

Publicly, Luce took an environmental position which was merely symbolic since privately Con Edison challenged the pollution regulations. Gains by the city in reducing emissions were made because of the city's strict regulations concerning the sulfur content of fuel, not by any initiative of Con Edison.

Opponents of the Astoria expansion contended that the real reason Astoria was needed was to ease Con Edison's troubled financial situation. Astoria was a capital expenditure and therefore could be included as a basis for a rate increase, since the rate per KW is based partially on capital investment. This gave Con Edison greater incentive to build new power plants rather than to seek other alternatives.[107] Higher rates would in turn attract more capital, with which further investments could be made.

Another way to assuage public opposition was with benevolent activity, that is, by offering the community benefits which represented a small financial outlay for Con Edison. Soon after Con Edison publicly announced its plans for Astoria, it contacted Queens political leaders. For their support, Con Edison offered to beautify the community. Recreational facilities planned included a football field, a track field, a volleyball court, and a basketball court. In addition, Con Edison promised to remove its two unsightly gas tanks and construct a new fence and traffic entrance. Queens Borough President, Sidney Leviss, praised Con Edison's efforts to improve the community. Leviss seemed to have been won over and asked, "How many people would choose to eat in a non-air conditioned hotel or motel?"[108] "We have no other alternative but to supply the ever-increasing demand for power."[109] Political leaders offered no substantial opposition until Astoria residents organized to oppose Con Edison. Con Edison hoped that it would obtain community support because of its efforts to provide recreational facilities and to make the plant as unobtrusive as possible.[110] Such action was symbolic because it tried to increase the satisfaction level of the community with benefits quite unrelated to the real issue.

132

Con Edison's opposition to the Air Code's emission standards, stack emission regulations, and sulfur restrictions in fuel oil were stated in terms of saving consumer money to appeal to a financially overburdened public. Con Edison also projected itself as a company besieged by regulatory agencies. These two strategies were designed to relieve Con Edison of any negative effects of its actions and to upgrade Con Edison's public image.

The 1973 Fuel Crisis

Appeal to patriotism, another symbolic gesture, was implicit in Con Edison's proposal to burn coal as stated in its October 25, 1973 application to the city. Supporters of the variance argued that as a nation, less reliance should be placed on foreign sources of fuel. The strategy was designed to demonstrate the larger national benefits inherent in the variance. It supported the presidential theme of patriotic self-reliance and national self-sufficiency. The program corresponding to this national goal was to develop coal resources which were supposedly available nationally and which would be cheaper than oil. Con Edison claimed that coal would save 3.5 million barrels of oil from April 1, 1974 to December 31, 1974.[111] The best way to bring the world oil price down, and to reduce dependence on foreign oil sources, was to burn more coal.[112] Because coal was produced domestically, it was not subject to fluctuations in foreign policy. However, it was clear that if coal were to be used extensively, environmental laws would have to be relaxed.

The strategy of appealing to broad public goals was a second strategy used in support of coal. This argument had an economic rationale. If oil indeed was more expensive than coal, its use was a contributing factor to inflation since the consumer had to pay a higher price for electricity, which in turn pushed up the price for other goods and services. Tying electric power to economic prosperity during a time of unemployment and recession strengthened the argument. "The use of coal is certainly one means of relieving the financial hardships which have been placed on our customers."[113] At the March 1974 hearings, Con Edison claimed their fuel supply was insufficient because of the inadequate allocation of low-sulfur fuel by FEO, because of the oil shortage, and because it lacked desulfurization equipment. When additional testimony revealed that the oil supply situation was no longer critical, coal burning was then sought by Con Edison on economic grounds by claiming it would reduce the average consumer bill by 14% and reduce imports by $200 million per year.[114]

The coal strategy was an opportunity for Con Edison to attack the city's Air Code charging that it was too expensive. "We feel these authorities have not fully realized the enormous additional costs which our customers are being forced to incur in the interests of marginally cleaner air."[115] Con Edison referred to consumer outrage to electricity costs at the March 19, 1974 PSC rate hearings as reason to consider economic hardships of customers. However, Con Edison officials reminded the public that they were not abandoning clean air goals, but seeking a temporary relaxation of the regulations in the interest of the consumer.[116] By attacking the authorities and placing the responsibility of the high cost of electricity on them, Con Edison could demonstrate that it was concerned with the plight of consumers who were bearing the brunt of fuel costs because of the pass-through mechanism of any increased fuel charges. Con Edison argued that this financial hardship should be the basis for a variance to the Air Code. However, according to the Code, economic hardship could not be the basis of a city variance, and, as public knowledge, it must be assumed that Con Edison knew the city could not grant a variance on that basis.

Con Edison made contradictory statements to satisfy particular situations. It told the state that, in exchange for permission to use coal, it would use coal only for the time that oil was unavailable. Con Edison promised it would purchase the lowest sulfur content residual fuel oil reasonably available, work with the city and state for the best fuel use pattern, and enforce any conservation measures imposed.[117] However, in another statement, Luce argued that once coal was utilized, it would be best to continue its use because of the difficulties in securing a coal supply line and the high reconversion costs. He said Con Edison would ask PSC for financial compensation for the costs incurred from the conversion to coal-burning.[118] Thus, electric consumers would be paying for the costs of coal conversion. Con Edison Vice President Bertram Schwartz argued at the March hearings that only a long-term variance to burn coal was acceptable because the installation of desulfurization equipment could not be completed during the period of the proposed variance. Without a guarantee

134

of a long-term variance, Con Edison did not consider such
installation to be feasible. Schwartz testified: "In the
interests of long-term fuel reliability and flexibility as
well as in the interests of reduced energy costs to our
customers, we urge that you take such actions as necessary
to permit the long-term fueling of Arthur Kill #30 and
Ravenswood #30 with coal as the normal fuel."[119] Luce also
argued that the use of coal was not as harmful as CEPA
projected because the plants involved had high stacks and
because Arthur Kill could be converted to coal on short
notice, causing the least disruption to the Con Edison system.[120]
However, high stacks were never considered by environmentalists
as an air pollution control device and would not reduce
particulate emissions which result from coal. These
statements by Con Edison were symbolic since they ignored
realities or were contradictory with other Con Edison positions.
Con Edison thus minimized the environmentally negative aspects
in order to appeal to the broad public interest.

Higher Costs for Conservation

     At the time of the March 1974 hearings, PSC was also
conducting hearings on a proposed rate increase, and the
mood of the public at the time was hostile toward Con Edison.
The protests by consumers reinforced Con Edison's argument
that coal would represent an economic savings to the
consumer. Luce suggested again that irate consumers might
benefit if coal were used.[121] It is of interest that part
of the proposed rate increase that Con Edison was requesting
from PSC (6.7%) was due to the conservation efforts by the
public. Nevertheless, Con Edison argued that it needed an
increase in charges to bring revenues to the previous year's
levels.[122] The irony was that Con Edison was asking
consumers to pay for the electricity that was not used,
when consumers themselves were responsible for the energy
savings. In Con Edison territory, conservation efforts
did not economically benefit the consumer. The conservation
campaign by Con Edison was therefore a symbolic gesture
since consumers did not benefit for their conservation
efforts if they had to pay more in the end.

     In its public statements, Con Edison tried to show
concern for the environment. It said it had asked for coal
at the Ravenswood and Arthur Kill plants and not the
Astoria plant for environmental reasons. Closer examination
of the situation did not bear this out. At the November
1973 hearings, Con Edison said that if the crisis worsened,

135

it would request variances at other plants - including
Astoria. At that time, CEPA feared that if coal were
permitted at any Con Edison plant, the utility would later
try to expand the use of coal to the Astoria plant.
Fortunately for the city, a preliminary EPA report had
made it known that Astoria was unacceptable for coal-
burning and would never be allowed to burn coal, making
Con Edison's concessions not to burn coal at Astoria
worthless.

Image Building

In any dispute, a convenient strategy is to create
a scapegoat. The greater the emotional response of the
public, the more support can be created. Actors may
describe a situation as beyond their control and subject
to the whimsical actions of a conspiring enemy. Con Edison
cast itself in the role of an organization fighting to
keep costs down but beleagured by inefficient government
bureaucrats who were unsympathetic to its financial plight
and that of its consumers. In doing this, Con Edison
pointed out the culpability of the government whenever
possible. It even noted that some public schools still
burned coal and that the city operated incinerators that
had not been upgraded.[123]

The image of Con Edison as an organization willing
to fight government bureaucracy may have been intended for
its investors. As a privately owned corporation, by
utilizing natural antagonism between business and government, it tried to maintain an aggressive stance. Con
Edison was supported by PSC in its resistance to air
quality regulations if they were not in Con Edison's best
interests. The Chairman of PSC said, "It would be deluding
ourselves to fail to recognize that the air quality
program has aggravated and intensified the fuel shortage
problem, and I believe the immediate threat of disabling
shortages cannot be removed without applying reason in
the drive for cleaner air."[124]

After the Arab embargo on oil was lifted and oil
became more available, Con Edison continued to campaign for
the use of coal. The policy was justified as promoting
economic savings for the consumer. However, according
to government authorities, the Con Edison estimates of
savings through the use of coal were exaggerated. CEPA
estimated a savings of 40 cents per month, using the
figures of $37 to $40 per ton, while Con Edison calculated

the price of $31 per ton. Con Edison overestimated
savings by underestimating both the price of coal on
the present market and the amount of electric power they
anticipated purchasing from other sources.[125] The
burning of coal brought with it other problems. There
existed a shortage of trained labor, and both equipment
and stocks of coal were unreliable because of long-term
commitments to other users. Coal companies were currently
unable to meet their existing contractual obligations. (It
would have taken from two to five years to secure adequate
supplies of coal to meet Con Edison's anticipated needs
since shortages were being reported by other utilities.)[126]
These conditions would have forced Con Edison to rely on
an inflated spot market, i.e., coal left over after contracts
with long-term contract holders were filled. As it happened,
Con Edison experienced difficulty in securing coal for the
Arthur Kill plant during the time of the variance, and
was able to burn coal only for four days before the expiration
of the variance. Con Edison's position that the burning
of coal would benefit the electric consumer was unproven.
Con Edison's statements were aimed at convincing the public
that its interests were being considered and were more
characteristic of symbolic action.

It is puzzling as to why Con Edison continued to
pursue a policy of coal-burning at a time when so many
obstacles were present. Here are a few speculations:
(1) It was well known that Con Edison did have a cash-
flow problem at the time, and the use of coal would have
enabled the company to have some leeway in paying off old
debts. (2) It improved Con Edison's image to pursue a
policy that could save its customers money, even if the
policy was unrealistic. Even if coal had been cheaper,
however, it would not have saved Con Edison any money
directly because of the fuel rider pass-through, which
would have decreased the customer's bill. (3) The ability
to use high-sulfur fuel would enhance Con Edison's freedom
in the fuel market by allowing the utility to burn whatever fuel it could get the best deal on. Prohibiting
coal cramped Con Edison's maneuverability in the fuel
market. If high-sulfur oil were competing with coal,
Con Edison could hypothetically get a better price when
the price of either fuel decreased.

Hearings

The implementation of the statutory requirements for public
hearings on the part of government were symbolic gestures to

137

comply with the law. Time constraints shortened the
procedures involved in the hearing process. Both sets
of hearings on Con Edison's applications involved less
than the required period of public notice time.
Insufficient time to prepare questions and testimony
limited the effectiveness of the investigation.
Environmentalists complained of inadequate time to
prepare estimates of savings in electric power consumption
due to fuel conservation measures. Evidence of toxic
health effects and in-depth analysis of the dispersion
impact of SO_2 and particulates could have been submitted
had more notice time been given.[127] The hearings at
times became emotional as tangential issues were raised.
This increased the pressure to agree on a decision,
eliminating the opportunity to examine the issues fully.
For the most part, the information received at the hearings
was not particularly revealing. Although the hearings
provided an opportunity to directly confront Con Edison,
they fulfilled the function of legitimizing subsequent
decisions made by the environmental agencies.

Accompanying the variances issued by DEC and CEPA to
Con Edison were conditions which had the appearance of
tightening control over Con Edison's impact on the environment but which were more symbolic than real. Close examination of these conditions reveals that their overall effect
would be minimal. The PSC certification of insufficiency
prescribed no enforcement powers for these conditions.
Neither DEC nor CEPA possessed such authority, either.
PSC recommended to DEC the confirmation of Con Edison's
efforts to purchase power, the monitoring of its conservation efforts, and the forbidding of coal-burning when
adequate supplies of conforming oil became available.
No definition of the term "adequate" was given. DEC and
CEPA variance conditions were similar although the decisions
differed. Both required that if coal were to be used until
March 31, 1974, stack gas "scrubbers" would be installed.
This condition would not reduce pollution emissions during
the period the variance was in force because no time limit
was given to Con Edison for their installation.[128] The
DEC variance included the PSC conditions, but no mention
was made of how DEC was going to enforce the requirements
that Con Edison (1) encourage conservation; (2) burn the
lowest sulfur content fuel available, or (3) increase the
base-load generation capacity of its nuclear plants. No
standards for conservation were set, nor were procedures

for determining how vigorous Con Edison must be in securing
the lowest-sulfur content fuel rather than the lowest-priced
fuel. The high costs of installing flue gas desulfurization
equipment gave little incentive to Con Edison to comply with
the requirement to report on its feasibility and prepare
for its installation. Since New York City was a no-growth
area, the investment simply lacked promise of a monetary
return. Even before Con Edison submitted the report, it
was known that flue gas desulfurization equipment would
take longer to install than the period of the variance,
and the expense for such a short period would be prohibitive.[129]
In addition, a shortage of "scrubbers" for coal-fired plants
made any such requirement for their use incapable of being
met.[130] These variance conditions were symbolic in that
they satisfied both legal requirements and the public, but
carried almost no weight because of the absence of any
enforcement and oversight procedures.

Summary

As demonstrated in the Astoria controversy, the
environment was an issue that could be used by actors to
create support for a policy if it appeared that the environment was being protected. Electric conservation had broad
appeal. On the government's side it was primarily a
symbolic appeal since the variances issued did not mandate
that conservation measures be taken. Both the environmentalists and Con Edison publicly acknowledged that conserving electricity would help ease the fuel crisis.
The environmentalists hoped that the conservation of
electricity would lessen fuel needs and thereby minimize
the effect of pollution. Conservation of electricity would
also reduce the likelihood of fuel shortages by utilities,
for which Con Edison blamed the environmentalists.

Although EPA maintained that conservation measures
would have to be taken before any variance would be
given, no comprehensive conservation action developed.[131]
While Con Edison and the fuel industry used conservation
to dramatize the shortage situation to support the relaxation of air quality standards, the environmentalists used
conservation as a means to maintain air quality standards.
A situation developed where the participants, whose
objectives were antagonistic, advocated the same symbolic
policy.

139

Many actions taken in response to crisis situations are more legitimately attempts to increase public support than to reduce underlying conflicts. Often basic strategy is disguised with language appealing to broad public ideals to which all sides in a conflict can agree. The real decision may turn out to have less force and substance than suggested by official statements. Underneath the public layer of decision-making there existed in both the Astoria controversy and the 1973 fuel crisis a realm where the real decisions reflected competition between actors to have rules conform with their own programs and objectives.

> Proposition 6: The less concentrated the
> formal decision-making authority, the less
> is its influence on decision-making out-
> comes. Where there are unclear juris-
> dictional responsibilities, bargaining
> occurs to resolve these differences.

Fragmented policy-making in urban communities can be traced to institutional factors. Attempts to reform old machines by breaking up power through the establishment of pluralist mechanisms has, according to Theodore Lowi, had unfortunate consequences.[132] Power in many large cities is divided in such a way that the Mayor has little control of overall policy-making. Lowi cites examples of functional areas (e.g., welfare, water pollution, and civil rights) in which responsibility is divided among numerous city agencies, resulting in stalemated or conflicting outputs.

Where different levels of government share functions in one broad policy area, complex bargaining is one means of resolving differences. Sharing functions reduces the authority of an agency if the participants know that a decision may be subject to compromise on a different level of government. Agencies sharing functions may then search for a compromise that will satisfy all participants, and usually the participant with the greatest resources has the greatest influence in determining the outcome. If an ultimate or coordinating legitimating authority is absent, decisions made on one level of government in the same policy area may be inconsistent with decisions made on another level of government. Duplication of activity may not only result in inconsistency, but in spent scarce resources. When an issue is never completely resolved but

140

shifted to a different hierarchical level, both time and manpower can be wasted.

Agencies may choose to limit the boundaries of an issue to make the inevitable bargaining process more manageable. Limiting boundaries may also reduce the participation of some groups, thus enhancing the role of technical experts. Limiting the boundaries of an issue does not guarantee that the problem will be solved at any acceptable level. Therefore, although air quality standards may exist, continued inroads by granting variances to these standards will affect the overall policy of the national government to implement the goals of the Clean Air Act.

Another feature of the multi-jurisdictional policy-making which affects the bargaining process is the protective stance each level of government assumes toward its own prerogatives. States do not like to relinquish power to the federal government, and local governments like to maintain freedom when implementing policy directives from other levels. Moreover, since decisions made in one locality may affect a much larger region than the local area's legal jurisdiction, bargaining occurs on increasingly higher levels of government. In many policy areas there is no appropriate level of government at which a conflict may be resolved.[133] When solutions to problems cut across existing political jurisdictions and corresponding authority is absent, fragments of the problem will remain in the domain of numerous competing authorities.

The Astoria Controversy

The approval of the Astoria expansion proposal necessitated action from both energy-related and environmental regulatory agencies. While a few of these bodies had formal power such as the granting of permits, others assumed advisory roles. Agencies at the local, state, and federal levels were involved, and the absence of a coordinated policy or procedure made swift and definitive action on the Astoria plan difficult.

A brief summary of the positions of the environmental agencies illustrates the potential for conflict. The State DEC granted a water permit for construction following PSC approval of Astoria in its overall acceptance of

141

Con Edison's Ten Year Plan, which included the Astoria expansion.

Within the city government CEPA opposed the project while ICPU recommended approval. The ICPU report issued August 1970, (three weeks before the Mayor's decision) was a lengthy document, consisting of both a majority and minority section. The ICPU majority report acknowledged the importance of environmental constraints but was more concerned with possible power shortages faced by the city. Differing in priorities with the minority report, it noted that the city lacked the technical competence to evaluate either the capacity of Con Edison, its reliability or projected load estimates. City Administrator Kretchmer maintained in the minority report that Con Edison really did not need the Astoria plants, because there would be a surplus once the upstate plants were completed. The city's EPA maintained that there were 2,525 MW of reserve over the 20% requirement of the FPC, which brought the total reserve margin to 36% of demand. The minority report also claimed that there were alternatives to the construction of a plant within the city. Although Con Edison currently purchased 1,200 to 1,500 MW per year, they had omitted this source for estimation of future supplies. The minority report suggested that Con Edison develop its plans for plants on David's Island and Verplanck, sites already belonging to Con Edison. The report suggested that the old units scheduled for retirement, be held until 1974, when new sources of power would be made available. These older units, using .37% sulfur fuel, emit less sulfur oxide (6,300 tons or about 5.7% of total emissions in the city) as compared with 15,000 tons expected with a 1,000 MW plant (about 14% of total emissions). The minority report also maintained that, even with .37% sulfur fuel, federal minimum standards for air quality in the Bronx and Queens would be surpassed. Delaying the retiring of older plants would be a temporary commitment to the use of fossil fuel plants in the city.

On the federal level, NAPCA recommended that no additional plants be built in New York City because sulfur oxide levels near the East River were already double and triple contamination criteria. "From a community health point of view, therefore, it is undesirable to locate this plant in an area of already high...emissions."[134]

142

NAPCA's position was strong and direct in its opposition
to the Con Edison proposal. NAPCA was concerned that
since nine of the twelve city plants are located on the
East River and that Astoria itself was surrounded by
three Con Edison plants; and that the wind direction one
third of the time parallels the river causing the plumes
from these plants to intermingle that the emissions in
the area were already so great to impede the ability of
the air to disperse existing pollutants. NAPCA contended
that any additional generating plant should be built outside
the city as part of an overall effort to reduce emissions
in the city.

Fragmented Authority

        The actual environmental opposition to Astoria was
based on the potential hazards of increased air pollution,
although at that time there were no federal emission
standards for stationary sources for Con Edison to conform
to.   The city's legal power to block Astoria was not based
on specific air pollution regulations, but on approval of
various permits (i.e., Fire Department, Department of
Buildings, and Department of Ports and Terminals).   The
power of the city lay only in denying permits which were
non-environmental in nature. (The only environmentally
related permit was for boiler installation from the DAR.)
The permits were so limited in scope that if the particular departmental regulation was met, there was little
room for discretion by the agency.[135]

        The federal air quality standards that were promul-
gated in 1970 required enforcement by the state and were
incorporated into the State Implementation Plan (SIP),
but opinions in CEPA and DEC differed as to whether the
Astoria expansion would prohibit New York City from
meeting those standards. Without agreement on the effect
of the new generating facility, agreement on policy was
made more difficult. Legally, the city could impose
stricter standards than the state or federal government.
Although this gave the local government more control over
its air quality as well as responsibility for enforcement,
it also left the locality open to pressure from other
levels of government.

Lacking any authoritative power, the EPA position was to leave the matter up to DEC and Con Edison, hoping they would strike an agreement and figure out how federal air quality standards would be met. Legally the EPA's only power was to request that the Army Corps of Engineers deny the permit on the basis of water pollution, not air pollution.

The city possessed no agency that dealt directly with electric power supply problems. ICPU held only advisory power and could not enforce any modifications of Con Edison's plans, nor could it even compel Con Edison to reply to ICPU objections. The city was therefore forced into a decision when the authority and responsibility really rested with state and federal authorities. ICPU acknowledged its limited powers in its report, saying that none of the city permits "go to the heart of the matter, i.e., whether the city consents to have a plant built within the city limits."[136] ICPU felt the state and federal governments should make the decision.

Although the city finally made a decision, which of course was incompatible with EPA recommendations, that decision could have been later modified by administrative procedures concerning state and federal discharge and construction permits. What occurred was a decisional process characterized by incompatible actions and occasional redundancy. It may be argued that this is not necessarily a harmful phenomenon because it allows additional time for review at different levels of govern- ment, which may bring forth new information. Nevertheless, without regularized procedures and clear jurisdictional lines of responsibility, ambiguity and confusion may predominate. If three regulatory agencies yield con- flicting judgments, the participant to be regulated can play one agency off against another by using the approval it gets from one agency as a basis for supporting its position to the others. Con Edison clearly tried to pressure both the city and EPA to change their opinions by using the approval they received from PSC and FPC.

Bargaining - An Example

The following anecdote illustrates the political pressure exerted by Con Edison toward NAPCA to force the reconsideration of its position. William Megonnell,

HEW Assistant Commissioner for Standards and Compliance, met with Con Edison officials on July 24, 1970. Con Edison said it would be able to reduce the sulfur dioxide emissions by two thirds from 1970 to 1976. The conversation, according to Megonnell, was frank, and Con Edison requested that its status be reevaluated by NAPCA in light of both the new data and the approval of its Ten-Year Plan by PSC.[137] On the same day Kenneth Johnson of NAPCA met with Con Edison at the regional office in New York. Victor Hanson of Con Edison told Johnson that NAPCA was reconsidering its opinion. Hanson distorted Megonnell's words, for Megonnell explained that he had only promised to reevaluate the new data. Con Edison tried to make it appear as if NAPCA was retreating from its previous position and would act more favorably toward the Astoria proposal.

On July 30, 1970, Harry Woodbury, a Vice-President of Con Edison, called Megonnell and suggested that if NAPCA was reconsidering its position, it should let the city know because action by the city was imminent. Woodbury also acknowledged receipt of the permit for two electric generating stations (boilers #60 and #70) from the Department of Air Resources, signed by the Action Officer and with Rickles' name stamped on it. Woodbury said he doubted if Rickles ever saw it.

On July 30, 1970, Woodbury told Megonnell that Luce had talked with the Governor and the Mayor and had received their written approval of the project. The Governor assured the Mayor he wouldn't "rock the boat".[138] He hinted that the Mayor was expected to make a public announcement on August 3, 1970. He suggested that NAPCA might want to change its mind since the decision might embarrass the "feds." (NAPCA would then be the only agency opposing the plant.) He further suggested that NAPCA's opinion was based on incomplete information.

At the same time, the Regional Office of NAPCA informed the city that it was reevaluating the new data. The city EPA was simultaneously pressuring the Regional Office for more data in opposition to Astoria, even if NAPCA withdrew its position. Megonnell noted that if the city cancelled its request for technical assistance, NAPCA would withdraw unless serious pollution was evident. When Rickles cancelled the boiler permit on July 31, 1970, he

145

told Woodbury it was because NAPCA objected to it. Since
NAPCA did not withdraw its opinion, we can safely assume
Rickles or Kretchmer continued to press for its aid.

The same day, Megonnell was informed that Deputy
Commissioner of Air Resources, Hart, denied that any permit
had been issued to Con Edison and said he knew nothing of
the Mayor's imminent decision. Mr. Fabricant, General
Counsel for CEPA, said the permit was not authorized to
be issued, but if it was, it would be an administrative
mistake and would be rescinded. It was also reported
that a Con Edison lawyer had advised CEPA through inter-
mediaries that NAPCA was reconsidering its position. CEPA
again asked the Regional Office for additional support
against the Astoria plant. This reevaluation by NAPCA
had become known to a New York Post reporter, who had been
given a letter by Dr. Shy of HEW giving detailed health
effects of the sulfur and nitrogen oxides involved in the
Astoria expansion. This was the evidence NAPCA would use
to substantiate its opposition to the Astoria proposal.
Since both CEPA and the Post reporter knew about this
reevaluation, NAPCA could no longer retreat from its stand.

At 5:30 P.M. that evening, Woodbury called Megonnell
and told him that Rickles had informed Luce that the
permit was being cancelled because of federal objections.
A telegram was allegedly sent to Con Edison revoking the
permit, according to Fabricant. Woodbury also wanted to
know what, if anything, NAPCA had told Rickles.

On August 1, 1970, Woodbury again called Megonnell's
home and said he was concerned about Luce's testimony before Senator Muskie's Joint Committee on Atomic Energy.
He asked for NAPCA's advice. Woodbury reminded Megonnell
that NAPCA's original position was based on incomplete data.
He noted that the impact of nitrogen oxides would be
difficult to ascertain because of the numerous mobile
sources in the area. Woodbury said that Kretchmer was
putting the Mayor in a difficult position. "Kretchmer
is attacking the Mayor. He submitted a minority report
after Lindsay's mind was made up. The politics appear
to have become heated and NAPCA is being placed in the
middle." Woodbury also inquired how much Kretchmer
knew. Perhaps he was asking NAPCA not to give Kretchmer
any more ammunition which would embarrass NAPCA if the
Mayor approved. Pumping Megonnell for information might

146

have been a way to help Con Edison influence the Mayor's decision. Although NAPCA was placed in a difficult position by the pressures exerted by Con Edison, NAPCA officials did not change their position after the plant size was reduced to half by the Mayor, and it consistently and adamantly opposed the Astoria expansion.

These events illustrate how pressure tactics are used to influence outcomes where jurisdictional responsibilities are unclear. Con Edison attempted to play one agency off against the other to maximize its position while at the same time it shifted its focus to higher governmental levels.

The state decisions to approve the Astoria proposal were not based on any clear procedure for power plant siting because none existed. There was no formal mechanism for the inclusion of environmental concerns in the PSC approval for new power plants. Long-term delays encouraged utilities to argue for streamlined procedures. Con Edison would have preferred a one-stop power plant siting process, making it easier for an agency to pressure local communities into approving a project. The lack of a concise policy toward power plant siting by power and environmental agencies was an important factor which resulted in open disagreement and conflict.

Another jurisdictional problem which occurred concerned pollution across state lines. NAPCA recognized that New Jersey standards were more stringent than those of New York. "No action should be taken in New York that in any way jeopardizes the opportunity for a neighboring state to achieve their air quality goals."[139] New Jersey had a real interest in the effects the Astoria project would have on New Jersey air quality, but lacked any role in the decision-making process. Only EPA had broad enough jurisdiction to consider the total region, although its formal powers were limited to recommendations.

When a decision-making body lacks the authority to control the implementation of its own regulations, there is an impetus toward reconciliation with the positions of the other actors. The city decision was clearly such a case; by cutting the proposed Astoria expansion in half, the Mayor tried to resolve the conflicting recommendations of federal and state regulatory agencies through compromise.

147

The 1973 Fuel Crisis

During the 1973 fuel shortage, similar problems were encountered which continued to produce jurisdictional overlap and discoordinate positions. Environmental and power regulatory agencies again came into conflict over how the city would deal with the fuel shortage that Con Edison was experiencing. Although the city was responsible for implementing the SIP as it applied to city air quality laws and regulations, city procedures incorporated in Local Law 49 for variances differed from state regulations and were more stringent. Although CEPA was designated as a local agent of the state, the city claimed its jurisdiction was separate from the state.[140] When the City and State drafted their separate decisions, they were surprised by the differences between them.[141] An agreement with the city stipulated that the stricter rule would always apply.[142]

The Decisions

Specific provisions for variances from the air code (Local Law 49) differing from DEC regulations (Section 226 of NYCRR) were: (1) while the state had no restrictions on the length of time for a variance, the city could legally grant a maximum six-month variance; and (2) DEC could grant a variance based on economic hardship while the city was limited to "undue hardship" conditions. DEC adopted the CEPA position after the March 1974 hearings, when Con Edison's application was based primarily on economic factors, that is, when it argued that its consumers were being subjected to unnecessarily high costs for low-sulfur fuel.

Divided Opinion

Varying perceptions of risk resulted in different decisions on three levels of government. The November 1973 decisions by CEPA, DEC, and EPA granted Con Edison variances with dissimilar provisions for the use of coal and high-sulfur oil. The CEPA decision gave Con Edison a six-month variance to burn 3 million barrels of non-conforming oil with a sulfur content of 3%. It prohibited the burning of any coal at Arthur Kill #3 and Ravenswood #3. The DEC exception to the SIP gave Con Edison permission to burn an unlimited amount of 1.5% sulfur content oil for a period of one year and to burn 300,000 tons of coal (equal

to 1.85% sulfur content oil) at Arthur Kill #3 and Ravenswood #3. Limits on oil would be increased to 3% sulfur
content if the more stringent requirements could not be
met. EPA opinion allowed coal only at Arthur Kill #3
because of its short conversion time,[143] and residual oil
of up to 1.5% sulfur content oil at Ravenswood #3 and up to
3% sulfur oil at Arthur Kill. The EPA emphasized that
the conditions imposed by the state variance be enforced,
especially regarding efforts to obtain stack gas "scrubbers."[144]

CEPA was disappointed by the DEC action permitting
the use of coal and unlimited amounts of non-conforming
oil. CEPA disagreed with both the EPA and DEC opinions
that air quality standards would still be met. DEC had
been under pressure by the November 23rd PSC certification
of the unavailability of conforming fuel. PSC said the
certification was based on the November hearings, on facts
presented by Con Edison in its application, on additional
information submitted in response to questions raised at
the hearings, and on public information. Because of cur-
tailments of anticipated deliveries, Con Edison estimated
its shortfall at a minimum 4.2 million barrels of conforming
oil and 2.1 million barrels of non-conforming oil even if
the sulfur restrictions were lifted. According to Con
Edison testimony, conservation efforts could save as much
as 2 million barrels during the period of the variance.
PSC concluded that, although low-sulfur fuel oil might
become available, the possibility of shortages did threaten
reliable electric power generation, resulting in reserve
storage being exhausted in 2 months, with resulting black-
outs and threats to the health and safety of the city.
PSC recommended the reconversion of Arthur Kill #3 and
Ravenswood #3 to coal as quickly as possible. Because
coal companies require long-term contracts, Con Edison
would need to burn coal for at least a period of one
year. PSC appreciated the effect of burning non-conforming
fuel on air quality, but felt that health aspects must be
balanced with the special and economic effects of rotating
neighborhood black-outs. Conditional to the variances
recommended by PSC, Con Edison was informed that it must
(1) pursue its contractual arrangements with its suppliers
regarding committed volumes, grades and values of oil;
(2) make efforts to obtain conforming oil to meet its
needs; (3) transfer any savings incurred through the use
of non-conforming fuel to its customers; (4) encourage
conservation measures in its own operations and among its
consumers; (5) attempt to increase the purchase of power

from outside sources; (6) end the use of coal when adequate supplies of conforming fuel became available and its coal supplies became exhausted; and (7) make monthly reports to PSC and DEC Commissioners during the period of the variances regarding implementation of the above conditions.[145]

As discussed earlier, varying perceptions of risk can be a contributing factor to the differences in authoritative decisions. Had DEC denied an exception to the SIP and electric power shortages resulted, DEC would have been held responsible on the state level. Since DEC could not disapprove the PSC finding, it enjoyed little discretion in reaching a decision. Since the city had no certification of insufficiency regulations, CEPA had one less constraint to consider and thus more maneuverability. EPA's opinion was based on the FEO assumption that East Coast shortages would occur even with conservation measures.

After the November 1973 decisions, the city felt pressure from governmental agencies as well as by Con Edison to modify its decision. EPA advised the city that its permission to allow coal at Arthur Kill #3 depended upon the city's going along with it.[146] Meanwhile, Con Edison said it would begin conversion to coal at Arthur Kill #3 even without permission from the city.[147]

Con Edison continually used its influence at higher levels of government to change city and state decisions. Con Edison went directly to EPA headquarters and FEO to complain that EPA Region II had denied it coal at Ravenswood #3 and that they would soon run out of oil.

Lack of federal direction also weakened the city's position. Not only did DEC and EPA pressure CEPA to allow coal, but Con Edison and the oil companies complained they were having difficulties obtaining oil. FEO was besieged by city and environmental groups pleading for the allocation of low-sulfur fuel for New York City - without much success. Without a definite commitment from FEO that it would allocate oil to the city, CEPA was forced to allow coal. The city hoped that FEO would ban coal for Con Edison facilities when it published its list of plants which would be allowed to convert to coal. Although EPA could oppose the use of coal at a specific

150

plant, FEO was still in a position to force conversion to coal by holding back on oil allocations, and EPA had no power whatsoever regarding the distribution of oil. For a time, EPA and FEO had policies which were in direct conflict with each other.

Conforming to the 1970 Clean Air Act was another area of potential conflict between the two federal agencies. The proposed Emergency Petroleum Allocation Act did not mandate that low-sulfur fuel would be allocated to the Northeast area, a policy which FEO had not yet supported. This would make it difficult for some areas to meet air quality standards. Although the Emergency Petroleum Allocation Act did state that FEO had an obligation to conform to the Clean Air Act, environmentalists were fearful that relaxation in the standards would occur.

Con Edison on occasion tried to make use of the fragmented and uncoordinated political system to eliminate restrictions on the use of coal. On January 1, 1974, Woodbury told the city that Con Edison was unable to purchase low-sulfur coal as required by the variance, and had secured an agreement from DEC Commissioner James Biggane for an emergency exception to use higher sulfur coal. Con Edison also sent Elish (CEPA) a telegram asking permission to use higher sulfur fuel in the light of its appeals to EPA for coal at Ravenswood. The telegram read: "/If/ granted and assuming your permission to burn coal at this plant is also received, our need for coal will be greatly increased, our need for the permission...becomes more critical."[148] Reserves of oil were down to 9.8 days and Con Edison wanted immediate approval to burn coal. However, a call on Janaury 14 to DEC Assistant Commissioner Steve Gordon in New York City revealed that a variance had not been agreed upon. Elish then called Biggane and learned that Biggane had said only if Con Edison were unable to obtain low-sulfur coal would an exception be issued in the future. Subsequently, CEPA staffer, Larry Chertoff contacted suppliers of coal for Public Service Electric and Gas of New Jersey for information on coal supplies, since there were no central sources of regional information regarding price, supply, or quality. A few days later, a list of sources on low-sulfur coal was made available to Con Edison. The company then dropped its request for high-sulfur coal, explaining that the coal situation had changed for the better over the prior 5 days.

151

The Situation Changes

By the time of the March hearings (to determine if the variances held by Con Edison and the oil suppliers should be extended), government agencies had developed cooperative working relationships with each other. The decisions of agencies reflected increased analysis of the oil supply situation and impact of non-conforming fuels upon the air quality of the region.

On March 27, 1974, DEC granted exception from 6 NYCRR Section 225.2(d) and (b) to Con Edison for 1.5 million barrels of non-conforming oil per month for the duration of the PSC certification of insufficiency but only if prior evidence submitted by Con Edison indicated that conforming oil was unavailable. In denying the use of coal at Arthur Kill and Ravenswood, DEC Commissioner Biggane discounted the economic savings as irrelevant. (DEC had asked Con Edison on March 11 to substantiate the price differential which was to yield the economic savings, but Con Edison had failed to address that request.) Con Edison was allowed to keep the coal it had acquired in storage until December 31 or until FEO decided which utilities could use coal. Biggane noted that the utility demand for power had not increased and that availability of oil made the future more optimistic. "This conclusion is supported - and in fact - required by Chairman Swidler's certification of an insufficiency of conforming fuel only" stated the DEC decision and no shortage of non-conforming oil was demonstrated.[149] DEC added a provision that any savings resulting from lower fuel costs must be passed on directly to the consumer. Biggane reserved the right to consult with the PSC Chairman to determine sufficiency of fuel supplies so that the exemption for limited use of non-conforming oil could be revoked.

CEPA released its decision on March 29, 1974. It was based on the changed fuel supply situation, which indicated that all of Con Edison's suppliers would be able to deliver conforming oil. As for coal, the price per ton had increased, while the price of oil had stabilized, thus dealing a blow to Con Edison's economic-savings argument. CEPA estimated the savings would amount to only 40¢ per month. The city also considered the FEO report, which characterized the use of coal at Arthur Kill and Ravenswood as an environmental hazard. Although annual average air quality levels were not greatly affected by non-conforming fuel, these standards were not presently being met. Special concern was expressed about the effect on the 24-hour average. Moreover, if a plant's precipitator should fail, the effect on ambient air quality would be disastrous. Therefore, the city forbade the use of coal and non-conforming oil unless both a written statement from the supplier indicating inability to deliver conforming oil and a statement from Con Edison detailing the shipment and efforts to secure conforming oil were supplied. The Administrator would then make the final decision. This conditional variance applied until June 30, 1974, and set the limit at no more than 1.6 million barrels of oil with a sulfur content of no more than 1%. The application to burn coal beyond March 31, 1974 was denied. Con Edison was permitted to maintain in storage the coal in its inventory, but it had to apply for further variances to burn it.

On March 27, 1974, PSC published a report by Alan Roth, Executive Assistant to the Chairman of PSC. He explained that the situation had changed because the federal mandatory allocation program could now supply oil to New York City. Russell Train, EPA Administrator, and William Simon, FEO Administrator, wrote suppliers on January 16, 1974, asking them to voluntarily ship low-sulfur oil to New York City. Con Edison's energy conservation program had also reduced electric demand by 10% (a possible result of PSC prohibition of energy sales promotion and a 5% statewide voltage reduction). Without federal approval, Roth said the state could not authorize further use of coal: however, if the federal government did approve it, the state would then find it difficult to prohibit its use. Since Con Edison was now asking for coal on grounds of economic relief, not insufficiency of oil, the analysis by PSC had to be different.

Since all suppliers indicated they would be able to meet their obligations, Roth recommended to the DEC Commissioner (1) to consider the economic advantages, and (2) to authorize coal unless serious health effects could result. Conditional to the use of coal, Con Edison should be required to: (1) attempt to secure adequate

153

supplies of conforming residual oil; (2) pursue contractual entitlements to volumes, grades and values of oil;
(3) pass savings on to customers; (4) maximize efforts
to conserve fuel in its own operations and with customers;
(5) continue the purchasing of power; and (6) report
monthly to the PSC Chairman and the DEC Commissioner
for the duration of the certification.

Summary

Unclear lines of responsibility, jurisdictional
overlap, and multiple decision-making centers thus
resulted in conflicting policies. These conditions
made it more difficult for each individual environmental
agency to fulfill its mandated responsibility. Conflict
was resolved in competitive bargaining situations which
compromised agency standards and goals. This changed
when procedures for issuing variances were routinized
and jurisdictional responsibilities became clearer.

> Proposition 7: Multiple authorities trying
> to control the decision-making process
> may provide occasions for innovation;
> crisis situations may create opportunities
> to innovate by broadening the scope of
> the issue and by adding new resources
> and participants.

"The innovative decision arises from a willingness
to accommodate some internal and external pressure incompatible with a central element or organizational
character or from a drive to deflect such a demand and
preserve the status quo."[150] Innovation during crisis
situations does not usually provide for extensive policy
changes, nor for modification of routinized patterns of
agencies dealing with their constituencies. However,
the very constraints of a crisis situation may temporarily
provide the opportunity for innovative behavior after
the crisis subsides. Innovative behavior, which may be
thought of as the generation and implementation of new
ideas, processes, and products or services,[151] may be
an unanticipated by-product of decision-making under
crisis conditions. The public attention that a crisis
creates often encourages young administrative agencies
to assume an aggressive role in the aftermath.

The Astoria Controversy

As a young agency, CEPA took on a crusading aura
during the Astoria controversy, a characteristic usually
associated with "young, open, nontraditional agencies."[152]
The first major issue confronting CEPA was the Astoria
expansion proposal. What the staff lacked in expertise
and experience it compensated for with zeal, determination,
and the self-confidence with which to take on a challenge.
Mayor Lindsay gave CEPA enough freedom to develop a
sense of independence. Environmentalism was an issue
he supported, and therefore CEPA was prepared to use all
available resources if it was determined that Con Edison's
proposal had a detrimental environmental impact.

Although Con Edison did not enjoy a good public image
due in part to widespread complaints about its service, no
governmental body had ever forced Con Edison to justify
its actions. PSC granted Con Edison rate increases based
on Con Edison's own analysis of its financial situation
and did not include environmental costs in the determination
of rates. In the Astoria controversy, CEPA hoped to
force Con Edison to be more responsive to environmental
matters and to add environmental concerns as an element
of the decision-making process for power and energy issues.
To this end, CEPA used every possible resource to push dis-
course into the public arena, thus removing debate from
the private agendas of City Hall and Con Edison.

Virtually overnight, CEPA staffers had to become
educated in the fields of electric power generation and
energy policy. Organizational lines were not fixed, and
staff within CEPA were transferred from department to
department within CEPA whenever they were needed. For
example, Administrator Kretchmer drafted program analysts
from the Sanitation Department to help formulate policy.
The Legal Office handled much of the communication with
Con Edison. Working closely and pooling their information,
the investigation and research done by CEPA staffers
became the basis of the Minority Report of the Interdepartmental Committee on Public Utilities (ICPU), which
was forwarded to the Mayor. Even after the Mayor made
his decision, continued interest in the problem led to
a more detailed study on the environmental consequences of
electric generation. "Toward a Rational Power Policy:
Reconciling Needs for Energy and Environmental Protection

was submitted to ICPU in April 1971. Its authors were Neil Fabricant and Robert Hallman, both legal counsels in CEPA. They attempted to broaden the issues which were generated by the Astoria conflict. Page 12 of the report summarizes their recommendations: (1) formulation of a rational energy and environmental plan for the State by a 15-member Temporary State Commission on Energy Needs, the Public Interest, and the Environment; (2) representation by environmental, health and community interests on any electric plant siting commission; (3) prohibition of continued encouragement of electric use; (4) encouragement of more utility funds for research and development; and (5) greater enforcement of pollution control standards.

Crisis situations often result in the creation of new authoritative entities. Realizing that the city lacked a governmental body to evaluate the Astoria proposal, Mayor Lindsay established the ICPU in 1969. In May 1970 it was formally asked to make a written report on the Astoria problem. ICPU was headed by the Municipal Services Administrator and included the Corporation Counsel, the Deputy Mayor, and Administrators of CEPA, the Economic Development Administration, and the Department of Consumer Affairs. The initial meetings of ICPU generated much argument among its members. Its final report gave approval to the Astoria proposal, leaving environmentalists in the minority of a 3-to-2 decision. The tremendous pressure brought about by CEPA led the Mayor to then open the issue to public debate, before he made his final decision.

The original 1970 Memorandum of Understanding with Con Edison, embodied in the Mayor's August 22, 1970 decision, designated ICPU as a permanent body responsible to the Mayor. Its primary objective was to oversee the implementation of the Memorandum. In succeeding months ICPU tried to broaden its mandate by making itself the only city body concerned with public utilities and fuel supplies. It subsequently hired a utility expert, Dr. Charles Lawrence, as a consultant to provide technical analysis. Subsequent ICPU annual reports analyzed the city fuel situation and the impact of national fuel policies on the city. It advocated the federal allocation of low-sulfur fuel to cities anticipating shortages in the low-sulfur fuel market. ICPU was increasingly concerned with Con Edison's ability to meet electric consumer demand in New York City; their progress in purchasing power, increasing transmission capability and conserving power.

Unless it is perceived that new ideas will be adopted, they will not be generated. For a brief time, CEPA was able to focus the attention of the public on the environment. As a result of the city's being thrust into a decision-making situation, the city acquired a measure of competence to deal with the environmental impact of electric power generation and focused the debate on broader questions such as slowing the growth rate for electric power. CEPA (1) questioned the present electric rate structure which encouraged greater usage; (2) suggested alternatives such as taxing inefficient electric appliances; and (3) established a relationship with the Power Authority of the State of New York (PASNY) for purchasing power on a regular basis and for allocating greater resources to pollution control research. CEPA made the environment a salient issue. The continued interest of CEPA in these areas left a residue of expertise when the issue of sulfur variances arose in 1973.

The 1973 Fuel Crisis

Although one positive result of the Astoria controversy was that it produced experience in environmental and electric power problems within CEPA, the city still lacked an effective arm for dealing with Con Edison. Lacking a crisis situation, CEPA did not undertake comprehensive analysis of the problems of fuel supply or of Con Edison's fuel supply procedures. Neither did any other city agency take up the question of limiting the environmental effect of continued power growth. Without the pressure of an important issue, the city shifted its attention from the electric power/environment question.

In the fall of 1973, the Municipal Services Administration (MSA) set up a board to deal with fuel supply problems concerned primarily with distribution within the city. The narrow perspective of the board led to underestimation of the consequences of a major fuel shortage. No city agency developed any form of general plan to maintain environmental safeguards for the city should a fuel shortage occur. The city had neither an energy policy for crisis situations nor proposals for broader objectives, including questions of electric power demand and continued growth.

157

CEPA became immediately concerned with the issue of the fuel shortage in the fall of 1973 because it was specifically asked to grant a variance to Local Law 49 at the request of Con Edison. The process of evaluating the application and deciding whether lower polluting oil was in such short supply that it necessitated the use of coal and high-sulfur oil required an intensive educational effort for CEPA staff members who were unfamiliar with variance procedures. This close-knit group of decision-makers consisted largely of CEPA people who had been trying to gather data about general energy supplies since late October 1973. The members of the Emergency Energy Supply Task Force, as it was soon named, met almost daily and were in close communication with each other. CEPA Administrator Herb Elish was particularly dependent upon these staffers because of the complex technical issues involved. Their duties included monitoring, on a continuing basis, all deliveries of non-conforming oil to the city, and the establishment of future needs for the city and for Con Edison specifically. They reported weekly to the Mayor on the availability of fuel and estimated needs; and they were required to notify the Mayor when needs exceeded supply. They were also responsible for providing information to the Administrator when requests for variances to Local Law 49 were made in order to maintain adequate fuel supplies.[153]

The experience gained by CEPA staffers enabled the city in subsequent variance hearings in March 1974, to more effectively analyze Con Edison's fuel supply situation. Those who had been concerned with Con Edison in prior months had now developed a critical attitude toward the utility and lobbied for reforms entailing more oversight procedures for Con Edison.

In order to internalize policy conflict in Mayor Beame's administration, Administrator Elish proposed early in January 1974 that a special Energy Office be established headed by a Deputy Mayor and a special assistant acting as an energy coordinator with a separate staff. Elish recognized that the city was forced to make concessions in the approval of variances because of insufficient information, and should another fuel shortage occur and similar pressure be applied, reforms in administrative procedure would be helpful. Elish suggested that the new Energy Office have (1) a liaison with FEO to encourage

158

mandatory allocations of fuel, (2) a liaison with DEC and
EPA to coordinate variances and monitor Con Edison supplies,
(3) a section to deal with contingency planning, (4) a
legal section to advise on the drafting of variances and
to formulate responses to proposed regulations and
legislation, (5) a section devoted to acquiring information
on sources of supplies, shipment, production, and price,
and (6) a liaison with the New York City Congressional
delegation. Elish also proposed that informational seminars
be conducted by John Lichtblau of the Petroleum Research
Foundation. MSA Administrator John Carroll forwarded a
similar recommendation to Mayor Beame, emphasizing that
the head of the Energy Office should have direct access to
the Mayor's Office and substantial authority in the city.
He suggested appointing a Technical Director who would
develop plans for coordinating inspections to oversee the
illegal use of non-conforming fuel, review proposed statutes
and rules for the impact of such fuel on energy supplies,
and advise on the subject of reducing energy consumption.
He also proposed that the legal section advise when
variances were required, and that a Public Information
Office be established to inform the public of the extent
of an energy crisis and the steps being taken to minimize
it.[154]

    The new Energy Office really never got off the ground.
It was to be staffed primarily by CEPA people, but only a
few of them ever moved into their new offices. Other than
devising emergency procedures for future energy shortages,
no one was clear about the new agency's specific function.
The jurisdiction between it and CEPA was never clearly
defined, creating confusion. Herb Elish, who, as the head
of the Energy Office, was directly responsible to the Mayor,
was also Commissioner of Sanitation - making him also
responsible to the CEPA Administrator. Moreover, the
Deputy Director was not highly regarded by CEPA staffers
because they felt he was a Beame political appointee, having
little interest in or knowledge of energy/environment
problems. By the spring of 1974, the Energy Office was
phased out and absorbed by CEPA. With the end of the fuel
crisis, energy problems seemed less critical, and the need
for further bureaucratic reforms became obscured. With a
change in City Hall administrations, the list of priorities
had changed.

The young, energetic public servants which the
Lindsay Administration attracted to city government
championed the goal of governmental responsiveness and
were idealistic enough to try to operationalize the
mission of their agencies. CEPA didn't fear reprisals
from the regulated agencies because they lacked the rapport
that established agencies enjoyed with their regulated
counterparts and had "nothing to lose."

The administrative reforms had only superficial
impact. Often innovative moves can not sustain momentum
after saliency of the issue declines. If bureaucratic
changes are not routinized before the crisis is resolved,
political pressures force reallocation of resources to
meet other exigencies.

Conclusion

The Astoria Proposal

Once Con Edison began construction of Astoria #6
with governmental approval, the question of city
regulation fell into obscurity. Nevertheless, the fate
of the Astoria #6 plant took an ironic twist. Because
of financial problems, on April 5, 1974, Con Edison
announced that it had offered to sell the partially
completed plant to the Power Authority of the State of
New York (PASNY). Discussions with the state regarding
such a sale had been held as far back as 1971, but the
reasons given for the sale then were problems because of
environmental opposition to construction of new power
plants. In 1974, Con Edison explained that cash shortages
due to high fuel costs could not be immediately recovered,
and an increase in overdue accounts receivable, forced
Con Edison to abandon the project. From 1967 to 1973, Con
Edison reported that its outstanding uncollected bills
(over six months) rose from $2.2 million to $3.4 million.[155]
Con Edison also had approximately $2.8 billion in capital
bonds outstanding, which forced it to issue new bonds at
the highest interest rates then charged to a utility because investor confidence had declined. On April 23, 1974,
Luce announced he would suspend its quarterly dividend
for the first time in the company's history.

160

The necessary legislation for PASNY to acquire from Con Edison, Astoria #6 (as well as Indian Point #3, which was purchased simultaneously) was passed by the New York State Legislature on May 17, 1974. It authorized the Authority to "Acquire and complete" facilities in New York City or Westchester County "to assist in maintaining an adequate and dependable supply of electricity by supplying power and energy for the New York Transit Authority, the Port Authority of New York and New Jersey, the City of New York, the State of New York, the United States, other public corporations and electric corporations within the metropolitan area of the City of New York..."[156] As of 1977, 76 government agencies have applied for power.[157]

The final sale to PASNY took place on December 13, 1974. The price PASNY paid for the Astoria #6 plant was $226,461,352, which represented the amount Con Edison had already spent on the plant. The transaction was financed by the sale of PASNY revenue bonds to the general public, since PASNY is prohibited from using tax money for projects. Con Edison may purchase up to 25% of the power produced at Astoria #6 in return for a Con Edison commitment to make available to PASNY, transmission and distribution lines. Astoria #6 finally began generating electricity on February 12, 1977. The plant for which Con Edison fought so adamantly is now being run by a state authority producing electricity at a cost lower than Con Edison could offer. Electric power shortages envisioned by Con Edison for 1974 never materialized, even without Astoria #6 being operational. Between late-1973 and mid-1974 actual consumption was below Con Edison estimates made prior to the Arab embargo, due in part to an increase in the price of electricity and conservation measures.

The events occurring during the period between 1969 and 1972 represent an interface between the private and public sector. Decisions by governmental authorities were made in response to action taken by a private utility. The Mayor's "Solomon-like" decision was an attempt to please both environmentalists and power adherents. What originally appeared as a routine decision-making situation became a major controversy for the actors involved and for the City of New York.

The 1973 Fuel Crisis

From the time of the passage of New York City's Air
Code in 1971, until the period under study, October 1973
to April 1974, Con Edison continued to publicize its
opposition to the air quality regulations. It first
argued that it could not get enough low-sulfur fuel to
meet those regulations, an argument which was plausible
during the Arab embargo. After the fuel shortage eased,
Con Edison argued that higher polluting fuels should be
used because they would represent an economic savings to
the consumer. The Arab embargo had only served to bolster
Con Edison's ongoing opposition to the city's Air Code.

During the fuel crisis of 1973-74, Con Edison began
reporting financial difficulties. Capital requirements
to support its program of modernization - $3.5 billion
between 1974 and 1979 - were not obtainable from private
markets.[158] Con Edison blamed its problems on increased
fuel costs and unpaid bills.[159] Con Edison also received
public criticism for its high rates, poor service, and a
discriminatory rate structure which favored heavy users.
In response, Con Edison argued that government regulatory
agencies and environmentalists were responsible for the
difficulties.

The ultimate decision of whether or not to grant
Con Edison variances during the fall 1973-winter 1974
period was influenced by pre-decision variables, that
is, a low-level of public information regarding fuel
supply or the impact of high-sulfur fuels on air
quality, multi-decision-making centers with overlapping
responsibility, and heightened public interest in Con
Edison operations and the environmental issues involved.
Environmental agencies were limited because of the city's
vulnerability regarding electric power. Chairman Luce
continued to threaten "draconian measures."

162

TABLE 2. Imports of Residual Fuel Oil by Percent Sulfur
          Content to New York State (thousands of
          barrels)[a]

	.0-.5	.51-1.00	1.01-2.00	over 2.00	total
Sept. 1972	8,604	1,075	1,677	2,788	14,144
Oct. 1972	8,511	1,318	1,357	2,411	13,597
Nov. 1972	9,899	1,289	1,046	3,023	15,257
Dec. 1972	13,083	1,447	868	3,372	18,770
Jan. 1973	13,821	990	1,317	2,389	18,516
Feb. 1973	11,605	2,046	436	2,381	16,467
Mar. 1973	13,531	2,132	400	3,242	19,305
Sept. 1973	9,215	274	469	3,969	13,927
Oct. 1973	9,806	274	975	3,601	14,651
Nov. 1973	12,236	460	1,951	3,667	18,313
Dec. 1973	9,174	850	2,902	2,520	15,446
Jan. 1974	9,551	780	3,490	2,876	16,696
Feb. 1974	9,279	1,494	2,583	2,789	16,145
Mar. 1974	8,286	1,218	1,023	2,707	13,234

[a]Source: Bureau of Mines, United States Department of
Labor

Although there was not a significant drop in overall oil imports to New York State from September 1973
to March 1974, deliveries of low-sulfur content conforming oil declined. However, considering the
tightness of the oil supply market, slight fluctuations
could have affected Con Edison if its suppliers failed
to deliver contracted supplies of oil.

The fuel crisis of 1973-1974 provided interests
in the private sector with an opportunity to manipulate
government regulators because of uncertainty in the oil
supply market. Con Edison exaggerated the situation
to fit its own purpose. The public sector was unwilling

to risk a power failure and unable to accurately assess
the lasting impact of the fuel shortage. Local political
leaders put together a strong coalition of forces in
support of the environmental position. More importantly,
local agencies lacked adequate resources to resolve a
problem whose origins were beyond the scope of New York
City politics.

CHAPTER IV

FOOTNOTES

1. Roger W. Cobb and Charles D. Elder, Participation in American Politics: The Dynamics of Agenda Building, (Boston: Allyn and Beacon, Inc., 1972), p. 26.

2. Regional Energy Consumption, A Joint Study by the Regional Plan Association, Resources for the Future, 1974, p. 11.

3. Con Edison System Planning Department, May 28, 1970.

4. Memorandum of Understanding between Con Edison and the City of New York, 1966.

5. Neil Fabricant and Robert Marshall Hallman, Toward a Rational Power Policy, (New York: Braziller, 1971), p. 207.

6. Letter from Louis Roddis, Vice-President, Con Edison to Milton Musicus, June 12, 1970.

7. New York Times, October 27, 1973.

8. Con Edison Public Information, October 26, 1973.

9. Letter from Charles Luce to John Love, October 25, 1973.

10. Letter from Con Edison Vice-President Harry Woodbury to CEPA Administrator, Herb Elish, October 26, 1973.

11. Letter from Charles Luce to DEC Commissioner Henry Diamond and PSC Chairman Joseph Swidler, October 25, 1973.

12. Ibid.

13. Schwartz testimony, Hearings held November 12, 1973, 2 World Trade Center.

14. New York Post, December 14, 1973.

15. CEPA Decision, January 4, 1974, p. 4.

16. Letter from Vice-President Harry Woodbury, Con Edison to EPA Regional Administrator Gerald Hansler, January 4, 1974.

17. Ibid.

18. Interview with Sally Streiter, September 22, 1975.

19. Letter from Con Edison to Robert Low, CEPA Administrator, January 29, 1974.

20. CEPA Decision, February 11, 1974.

21. Letter from Vice-President Harry Woodbury, Con Edison, to Robert Low, CEPA Administrator, February 20, 1974.

22. Con Edison Testimony, November 25, 1973, and Interview with Charles Komanoff, CEPA staff, December 29, 1975.

23. New York Post, February 1, 1974 and Memo from Eli Sadownick, Deputy Commissioner, DAR, to Herb Elish, CEPA Administrator, February 27, 1974.

24. Letter from Richard Weinand, NEPCO, to Bertram Schwartz, Con Edison, February 25, 1974.

25. Letter from T.N. Cook, Texaco, to Bertram Schwartz, Con Edison, February 22, 1974.

26. Letter from R.D. Zelik, Exxon, to Bertram Schwartz, Con Edison, February 22, 1974.

27. Letter from Phil Kramer, Amerada Hess, to Bertram Schwartz, Con Edison, March 4, 1974.

28. Testimony of John Sontowski, Assistant Director of the Bureau of Technical Services, DAR, March 11, 1974.

29. Interview with Charles Komanoff, December 19, 1975.

30. Testimony by Bertram Schwartz, Vice-President, Con Edison, March 11, 1974.

31. Freudenthal affidavit in response to questions at hearings, March 14, 1974.

32. Letter from Gerald Hansler, Regional Administrator, EPA, to Charles Luce, Con Edison, January 15, 1974.

33. Interview with Al Riesman, Regional Air Pollution Control Engineer, DEC, December 2, 1975.

34. Ruth Mack, Planning on Uncertainty, (New York: John Wiley), 1971, p. 5.

35. Letter from Charles Luce, Con Edison, to Mayor John Lindsay, July 22, 1969.

36. New York City's Power Supply, Development and Resources Corporation, October 28, 1969, p. 21.

37. Telegram to DEC Commissioner Diamond from Con Edison, December 12, 1970.

38. Con Edison Monthly Report on Generation and Transmission, PSC Case 25293, December 12, 1970.

39. Telegram to Harry Woodbury, Vice-President, Con Edison from DEC Commissioner Diamond, February 11, 1971.

40. Letter from Jacob Gelberman, Chief of Operations, Army Corps of Engineers to Con Edison, February 9, 1971.

41. Letter from EPA Deputy Regional Administrator Eric B. Outwater to DEC Commissioner James Biggane, October 10, 1973.

42. New York Post, November 20, 1973.

43. New York Times, November 26, 1973.

44. Ibid.

45. Ibid.

46. New York Times, December 3, 1973.

167

47. New York Post, December 6, 1973.

48. Letter from Con Edison Vice-President Harry Woodbury
     to CEPA Administrator Herb Elish, December 13, 1973.

49. Daniel Henning, "Environmental Policy and Politics:
     Value and Power Context," in Daniel Henning and Albert
     Utton (Editors), Environmental Policy (New York: Praeger,
     1973), p. 49.

50. Telegram from Con Edison to CEPA Administrator Herb
     Elish, January 11, 1974.

51. Letter from Vice-President Harry Woodbury, Con Edison,
     to EPA Regional Administrator, Gerald Hansler,
     January 4, 1974.

52. Testimony of Center for United Labor Action,
     November 12, 1973.

53. Testimony of Marcy Benstock, Clean Air, Inc.,
     November 12, 1973.

54. Letter from Vice-President Harry Woodbury, Con Edison,
     to Robert Low, CEPA Administrator, February 20, 1974.

55. Aaron Wildavsky, "The Strategic Retreat on Objectives,"
     Policy Analysis, (Summer 1976), II, Number 3, p. 515.

56. Aaron Wildavsky, Statement at Seminar, CUNY Graduate
     Center, October 18, 1977.

57. Wall Street Journal, August 21, 1970.

58. Intro. No. 380, Proposed Amendment to Section c 19-11,
     1c, New York City Administrative Code.

59. Letter to the District Engineer from Richard E. Griffith,
     Regional Director of the Bureau of Fisheries and Wild-
     life, February 23, 1971.

60. Letter to the WQO from Jacob Gelberman acknowledging
     request, February 19, 1971.

168

61. Letter from Jerome Kretchmer, CEPA Administrator, to Mayor John Lindsay, July 24, 1970.

62. Staff Report, PSC, prepared by Harold L. Colbeth, Sr., August 18, 1970.

63. Toward a Rational Policy, CEPA, op. cit., p. 8.

64. Interview with Sally Streiter, CEPA, September 15, 1975.

65. Letter from Deputy Mayor Edward K. Hamilton to William Simon, FEO, December 6, 1973.

66. Letter from Eric Outwater, Deputy Regional Administrator, EPA, to Harry Woodbury, Vice-President, Con Edison, January 22, 1974.

67. Press Release, CEPA, December 18, 1973.

68. Interview with Jim Marshall, Director of Public Information, February 12, 1976.

69. EPA Action Memo, March 25, 1974.

70. New York Times, September 12, 1973.

71. New York Times, March 22, 1974.

72. Letter from Herb Elish, CEPA Administrator to Alfred Kleinfeld, Acting Regional Director, FEO, January 10, 1974.

73. Draft Memo on Meeting with Con Edison from Ray Werner, Advisor, Air Programs Branch, EPA, January 3, 1974.

74. Letter from EPA Deputy Regional Administrator, Eric Outwater, to Harry Woodbury, Con Edison, January 21, 1974

75. John A. Straayer and Roy L. Meek (Editors), "The Iron Law of Environmental Disorder," The Politics of Neglect, (Boston: Houghton Mifflin, 1971), p. 241.

76. Murray Edelman, The Symbolic Uses of Power, (Chicago: University of Illinois Press, 1964), p. 38.

169

77. Ibid., p. 39.

78. Ibid., p. 27.

79. Statement of Mayor John Lindsay, August 22, 1970.

80. Ibid.

81. Letter from Charles Luce, Con Edison, to Mayor John Lindsay, July 22, 1969.

82. New York Times, August 10, 1970.

83. Letter from John Nassikas, Chairman, FPC, to Mayor John Lindsay, August 14, 1970.

84. Report by Harold L. Colbeth, Acting Director, PSC Electric Division, August 18, 1970.

85. New York Times, August 6, 1970.

86. Statement of Mayor John Lindsay, August 22, 1970.

87. Hearings before the Army Corps of Engineers, March 24, 1972.

88. Interview with Neil Fabricant, Counsel, EPA, September 25, 1975, and conversation with Bertram Schwartz, Vice-President, Con Edison, April 21, 1975.

89. Colbeth Report, op. cit.

90. "Environmental Impact of Con Edison Expansion of Astoria #6 – Comments on Draft of Impact Statement Prepared by U.S. Army Corps of Engineers, New York District," Bureau of Technical Services, DAR, July 26, 1973.

91. Roddis Letter, June 12, 1970.

92. Statement of Con Edison, Army Corps of Engineers Hearings, March 24, 1972.

93. Testimony of Roger Starr, Executive Director, Citizens Housing and Planning Council of New York, Army Corps of Engineers Hearings, March 24, 1972.

94. Testimony of Mr. Sternbeck, Executive Vice-President of New York Chamber of Commerce, Army Corps Hearings, March 24, 1975.

95. Testimony of Con Edison at the Army Corps Hearings, March 24, 1972.

96. Statement of Harry Woodbury, Con Edison, on the New York State Implementation Plan for the Metropolitan New York Area Quality Control Region, February 16, 1972.

97. Press Release, Testimony of Charles Luce at the City Council Committee on Environmental Protection, March 8, 1972.

98. Letter from Charles Luce, Con Edison, to Mayor John Lindsay, July 22, 1969.

99. Ibid.

100. Roddis Letter, June 12, 1970.

101. Letter from Austin Heller, CEPA, to Mayor John Lindsay, October 1, 1969.

102. Ibid.

103. Letter from Charles Luce, Con Edison, to Mayor John Lindsay, July 22, 1969.

104. Ibid.

105. Joint Hearings of CEPA, PSC and DEC, April 28, 1971.

106. Interview with Casimir Czarkowski, Engineer DEC, April 28, 1971.

107. Interview with Robert Rickles, DAR Commissioner, October 8, 1975.

108. Queens Ledger, Maspeth, New York, August 6, 1970.

109. New York Times, August 4, 1970.

110. Letter from Louis Roddis, Vice-President, Con Edison to Milton Musicus, June 12, 1970.

111. Daily News, January 15, 1974.

112. New York Post, January 15, 1974; Letter from Harry Woodbury, Con Edison, to Gerald Hansler, EPA Regional Administrator, January 4, 1974; Telegram from Bertram Schwartz, Con Edison, to William Simon, FEO, January 4, 1974; Letter from Harry Woodbury, Con Edison to Commissioner Biggane, DEC, January 7, 1974.

113. Telegram from Con Edison to CEPA Administrator Herb Elish, January 11, 1974.

114. Testimony of Vice-President Bertram Schwartz Con Edison, 2 World Trade Center, March 14, 1974. (Hereafter referred to as Schwartz Testimony).

115. Statement by Charles Luce, Con Edison, March 12, 1974.

116. Con Edison press release, March 14, 1974.

117. Letter from Harry Woodbury, Vice-President, Con Edison, to Herb Elish, CEPA Administrator, October 25, 1973.

118. Letter from Charles Luce, Con Edison to Henry Diamond, DEC, Commissioner and Joseph Swidler, PSC Chairman, October 25, 1973.

119. Schwartz Testimony.

120. Letter from Charles Luce, op. cit.

121. Letter from Charles Luce, Con Edison, to Russell Train, EPA Administrator, March 6, 1974.

122. Testimony of Vice-President Bertram Schwartz, Con Edison, Hearings, March 14, 1974.

123. Letter from Vice-President Harry Woodbury, Con Edison, to DEC Commissioner Biganne, PSC Chairman Swidler, and CEPA Administrator Low, March 21, 1974.

124. Speech of Chairman Joseph Swidler, PSC, before the National Conference on the Clean Air Act, Chapel Hill, N.C., November 1, 1973.

125. Interview with Jeff Cohen, Citizen's for Clean Air, September 15, 1975.

126. New York Times, November 12, 1973.

127. Interview with Marcy Benstock, Clean Air Campaign, Inc., April 7, 1975.

128. Statement by Eric Outwater, Deputy Regional Administrator, EPA, December 13, 1973.

129. Testimony of Edward Ferrand, Bureau of Technical Resources, DAR, November 12, 1973.

130. EPA Action Memo, March 23, 1974.

131. Speech by Russell Train, Administrator, EPA, before the Edison Electric Institute, EPA Seminar, Washington, D.C., December 3, 1973.

132. Theodore Lowi, The End of Liberalism, (New York: W.W. Norton, 1969), Chapter 7.

133. Dennis W. Ducsik (Editor), Power, Pollution and Public Policy, M.I.T. Student Systems Project (Cambridge, Massachusetts: M.I.T. Press, 1970), p. 18.

134. New York Post, August 3, 1970.

135. Report of the ICPU on the Expansion of Astoria, August 1, 1970, p. 2.

136. Ibid.

137. "Expansion of Consolidated Edison's Astoria Plant--New York City," Memo to Files, August 3, 1970, William Megonnell, NAPCA, Public Health Service.

138. Ibid.

139. Letter from Donald Walters, Director, Division of Abatement, NAPCA, to Ken Johnson, Director NAPCA, Region II, July 17, 1970.

140. Interview with Sally Streiter, September 22, 1975.

141. Ibid.

142. New York Post, November 27, 1973.

143. New York Post, December 13, 1973.

144. Statement by EPA Deputy Regional Administrator, Eric B. Outwater, December 13, 1973.

145. Report on Application of Con Edison of New York, Inc., under N.Y.C.R.R. Section 225.3(d), Dated October 25, 1973, Relating to Insufficiency of Fuel Supply, p. 33.

146. New York Post, December 13, 1973.

147. New York Times, December 14, 1973.

148. Telegram from Con Edison to Herb Elish, CEPA Administrator, January 11, 1974.

149. DEC Decision, March 27, 1974, p. 3.

150. William Gore, Administrative Decision-Making, (New York: John Wiley, 1964), p. 141.

151. Victor Thompson, Bureaucracy and Innovation, (Alabama: University of Alabama Press, 1969), p. 5.

152. Randall B. Ripley, "Policy-Making: A Conceptual Scheme," American Politics Quarterly, I, No. 1 (January 1973), p. 22.

153. Mayor John Lindsay Press Release, November 10, 1973.

154. Memo from John Carroll, MSA Administrator, to Mayor Abraham Beame, January 17, 1974.

155. New York Times, April 1, 1974.

156. Laws of New York State, Chapter 369, p. 506.

157. Telephone Interview with Ken Graham, PASNY, Public Information, September 29, 1977.

158. New York Times, April 1, 1974.

159. New York Times, April 5, 1974.

CHAPTER V

CONCLUSION

Focusing on the process of decision-making has provided the empirical basis for analyzing factors which limit political choices. The hypothesis of this study is that the type of decision-making occurring in a problematic situation not only affects the mode of conflict resolution, but the range of possible outcomes. The conflict between Con Edison and New York City concerning the environmental impact of electric power production may be viewed as one illustration of the generally inadequate response made by the public sector to environmental/energy problems.

In the two cases studied, incrementalism characterizes the decisional events. The seven propositions developed in the preceding chapter suggest the influence of variables that are characteristic of an incremental decision-system upon the authority of governmental actors and their relationships with the private sector under crisis situations. These propositions highlight the tenuous position of authoritative actors confronted with private sector participants with clear and precise goals and superior resources. The structure of American government and politics limited the bargaining resources of the governmental actors. This structure, together with ambiguities and conflicts of values in energy-environment issues and with crisis-related time pressures, determined city decision-making strategy well to the "incremental" end of the spectrum. Incrementalism weakened the influence of the city, giving Con Edison decided advantages because of the lack of clear definitions of the scope of the problem and intended goals, identification of suitable alternatives, and ongoing analyses and evaluation of current policies and programs.

Features of incrementalism - such as resolving conflict resolution through partisan mutual adjustment (bargaining), small moves made at the margin, serial moves, and the overlapping functions of multiple decision-making centers, intensify conflict among hierarchical levels of government and across agency lines. Incompatible decisions made by different government authorities are reconciled or tolerated.

176

Long-term goals are sacrificed for more immediate political and bureaucratic needs.

Tendencies encouraging incrementalism produced by the governmental structure are reinforced by the characteristics of energy/environmental issues. Because the technical level is unstable, requiring continual adjustments, and the public sector often lacks relevant information and technical competence, conservative action by local decision-makers is a favored strategy. Conflicts of both fact and value between energy and environmental goals heighten this effect.

Incremental decision-making has become more than an administrative procedure for decision-makers. It has been elevated to an accepted philosophy of twentieth century American government.[1] It is accepted because it is widely practiced. Breaking problems down into small manageable terms, however, precludes examination of their systemic origins. Incrementalism has thus shifted from being a behavioral description of decision-making techniques to a normative prescription of decision-making strategy for democratic government.

The first four propositions which compared levels of resources among actors illustrate the reinforcing nature of these factors. As the lack of control of information and the pressure generated by crisis situations limit the power of governmental actors, their impact on policy outcomes is diminished. Thus, the greater the crisis pressure the greater the value of available information becomes. If that information is controlled by the private sector, authoritative discretionary power and choice of options are limited.

Lacking long-term objectives, the government tends to act with ambivalence and in response to crisis situations through compromise with the private sector. Such compromises are unlikely to induce major change or promote problem resolution. The public sector's comparatively low level of resources is maintained because of the inability of fragmented government authority to intervene in a crisis without the support of outside groups. These mutually reinforcing tendencies perpetuate the recurrence of crisis because the systemic roots of environmental /energy conflicts are neglected. An incremental decisional strategy thus reinforces the characteristics of crisis decision-making.

177

LOW LEVEL OF RESOURCES ⟷ LOW DISCRETIONARY POWER

INCREMENTALISM

Observing decision-making styles on a continuum from rational-comprehensive to incremental, we find that incrementalism has been characteristic of environmental/energy issues in New York City. The outcomes of conflict have demonstrated the inability of the city to resolve these issues in other than a superficial or symbolic manner. It is suggested that solutions to environment/energy problems might be better handled by encompassing some of the attributes of the rational-comprehensive model, i.e., development of independent resources and planning activities.

"Bad" outcomes are not necessarily the result of conspiratorial persons, but the result of interests operating within a political subsystem able to fulfill their goals at the expense of other interests, which have fewer resources. Current decision-making in environment/energy problems reflects the configuration of local political power, where private actors (i.e., banks, business organizations, corporations,and developers) have an immediate stake in a governmental action which can be exploited by these actors as a public interest. Lacking a comprehensive perspective on environment/energy interactions, local decision-makers are subject to a myriad of pressures from groups able to express their specific interests with convincing thrust. Challenges to environmental values are made by groups using such concepts as economic growth, employment, and inflationary costs as justification for their views.

For example, in New York City, providing jobs and increasing corporate business and manufacturing activity is a major priority. In the eagerness to meet these objectives, little attention is given to the effect on the health of the city's residents that relaxation of environmental regulations can have.

The problem for local government is that institutional mechanisms do not exist for intervening in the cycle of

178

energy/environmental crises. New York City was unable to offer alternative solutions which would have provided adequate electric supplies with minimal environmental impact. Increasing the information resources of public authorities by establishing a permanent city body with sufficient expertise to monitor Con Edison activities - emphasizing scanning, analytic, and planning techniques - would increase the city's capability to enter the decisional process at a stage prior to the appearance of crisis, when the range of alternatives is minimal. Moreover, increasing the level of public input encouraged by public review of Con Edison plans, projections, and current operations would enlarge the sphere of conflict. Local community groups (i.e., Community Boards) have no effective access to Con Edison on issues that concern them. Communication between communities, their local legislators, and city officials could provide a source of support when needed by the city. If the public sector is to have an increasingly important role in decision-making in energy/environmental matters, changes will have to occur to increase the level of resources of authoritative actors to equalize their relationship with the private sector and to reform the tendency of decision-makers to deal with problems from a myopic perspective.

Much of the literature on policy-making and reform focuses on change. The impetus for change and its direction still remain undefined. The task now becomes one of defining desired goals and the means for achieving those ends. The political determination of priorities in a democracy, remains a critical problem.

The conflict between Con Edison and New York City concerning environmental impact raises a number of questions. How much public scrutiny is appropriate when the private sector has a monopoly over an important public function such as the production of electricity? Should building of higher stacks to disperse pollution from electric power plants be regarded as an acceptable solution to pollution, or should efforts be made to seek less polluting methods of production, or even changes in the demand for electric power? The search for answers may suggest new administrative procedures placing the planning functions of utilities under closer public control.

179

To meet the problem of breaking open the private, insulated decision-making structure of Con Edison, either (1) legitimized competing groups could be developed to counterbalance the power Con Edison exerts in the political arena, or (2) government might be equipped to become a genuine protector of the public interest. The first alternative would allow public interest groups greater access to the decision-making arena through continual consultation and inclusion in the decisional process, thus establishing a more competitive atmosphere. The second alternative would change the role of the government from a neutral regulator of competing interests to an active participant. This presupposes a coherent definition of public interest. It would legitimize governmental scrutiny over the private sector when a significant public function is at stake. The ultimate shift in this direction would be some form of public ownership of Con Edison – a policy which would enjoy support not only from those concerned about Con Edison mismanagement and high electric rates, but environmental hazards as well.

Proposals such as public ownership of Con Edison which would hopefully operate in the public interest require enormous sums of capital. Although electric rates may decrease somewhat, efficiencies of production are not automatic and ways would still have to be found to include the environment as a legitimate concern in decision-making. Nevertheless, as public dissatisfaction with Con Edison increases, greater interest may be taken in this alternative.

Genuine competition between government and private utilities might encourage private utilities to reduce rates through greater efficiencies. It has been shown that where competition exists, rates are lower.[3] In the spirit of competition, Westchester County Executive Alfred Del Bello, suggested that the county purchase its electricity from New England utilities or the Power Authority of the State of New York. Such proposals may initiate reforms by private utilities wishing to avoid greater regulation or loss of markets.

Beyond the question of public ownership of Con Edison, some more moderate suggestions may be offered to minimize the environmental impact of electric power generation.

Presently, the city has no regulatory function over Con Edison. The only way this can be changed is for PSC to delegate some of its responsibility to a city agency or to include representatives from the city in its procedures when actions concerning Con Edison are being considered.

Proposal 1

Since Con Edison still advocates the burning of coal and high-sulfur fuel in its system, the city might consider the formation of a permanent unit within the Environmental Protection Administration (now called the Department of Environmental Protection)   similar to the Emergency Energy Supply Task Force, but with a broader mission. Such a unit would have a permanent staff with expertise in electric power generation, including at least an economist, an environmentalist, and an energy specialist. It would work closely with the Bureau of Technical Resources to ensure that Con Edison was conforming to current Air Code regulations through on-site inspections of plants and continual monitoring of stack emissions. It would also monitor current fuel market conditions, with special emphasis on price and supply, as well as keep an inventory of Con Edison supplies. The unit would review plans submitted by Con Edison designed to meet emergency conditions if fuel supplies were interrupted. It would then impose penalties if equipment failed to meet performance standards. Finally, it would also approve emergency procedures for equipment failure.

Proposal 2

A more comprehensive arrangement that included most of the above functions would involve (1) the formation of a planning board with Con Edison representation (including its Environmental and Fuel Supply Departments) and (2) equal representation from the city. City representatives could be appointed by the Mayor with the approval of representatives from environmental and health groups and local legislators (i.e., councilmen or State senators) ensuring that the members chosen represented different communities of the city. The Chairmanship of the Board might be rotated or might be a permanent non-Board member acceptable to both Con Edison and the city. Members of the Board would be experts in problems of electric power generation and/or related environmental problems. All Board members must have access to Con Edison files and records. All long-range plans submitted to PSC would be first reviewed by the Board, as well as projections for meeting anticipated demand, the building of new facilities, integration with other electric power systems, and any agreements to which Con Edison was a party which would increase the utility's demand load. The emphasis would be on improving current production methods, committing funds, participating in the development of alternative sources of fuel purchase and power generation, and actively participating in all Con Edison decisions beyond internal corporate policy and financial ones.

Proposal 1 retains the present Con Edison-New York City relationship and has the advantages of keeping the city in an adversary position. Support from environmental groups could be maintained providing a means for active citizen participation. The city would be able to increase its level of resources to lessen the probability of crisis decision-making. In Proposal 2 the joint Board or Commission would be independent of current regulatory agencies. Working directly with Con Edison through the planning phases, it is at least theoretically possible that the city's involvement would increase. Conflict between the city and Con Edison could be reduced and the city would have a permanent role in all decisions involving electric power generation, i.e., environmental impact, electric rates, service to customers, and management efficiency.

Under any reforms, federal intervention would aid the city. In addition to local institutional reforms, federal policies such as allocating low-sulfur fuels to metropolitan regions during periods of shortage would relieve the city of potential pollution hazards. Not enough information is available on the long-range impact of fossil fuel combustion, which might be the focus of future federally funded research projects.

The thrust of these reforms emphasize public scrutiny, expanded decision-making procedures, tighter regulation where possible, greater public involvement, and an increasing role by the city in decisions involving the way electric power is produced. Although such changes suggest the barest skeletal reforms, they offer some direction toward which those concerned with environmental/energy conflicts

182

might gravitate. The objectives of such changes are to
increase the number of participants and the alternatives
open to government decision-makers. Public involvement in
planning and decision-making would discourage symbolic
action while increasing the level of resources of the
city equalizing the public and private sector.

Although the conflict between Con Edison and New York
City was of a localized nature, it highlights a basic
feature of energy/environment conflict in American politics,
i.e., that a common will is produced out of the interaction
of many discrete wills in the political arena. Because
there is no overall integrative mechanism directed toward
a recognizable goal, such outcomes in the political arena
may produce results considered undesirable by the community
as a whole. "What we really have is a congeries of uninte-
grated and competitive subsystems pursuing conflicting ends -
a non-system."[2]

Clearly, the response of political institutions that
resolve energy/environmental conflicts has been inadequate.
Any contemplated reform must reflect the values presently
neglected in considering the interaction of discrete wills
within the political process. To resolve differences
where energy and environmental values are predominant,
resources in the public sector must match the complexity
and urgency of environment/energy problems.

CHAPTER V

FOOTNOTES

1. William Ophuls, <u>Ecology and the Politics of Scarcity</u>
   (San Francisco: <u>W.H. Freeman, 1977</u>), p. 193.

2. <u>Ibid</u>., p. 189.

3. Richard Hillman, <u>Government Competition in the Electric
   Utility Industry</u> (New York: Praeger, 1972), p. 70.

BIBLIOGRAPHY

BOOKS AND PERIODICALS

Allison, Graham T. "Conceptual Models and the Cuban Missile Crisis," American Political Science Review, LXIII, (September 1969), No. 3, pp. 689-718.

Agger, Robert E. and Goldrich, Daniel. The Rulers and the Ruled. California: Duxbury Press, 1972.

Altshuller, Alan A. The Politics of the Federal Bureaucracy. New York: Dodd, Mead, and Co., 1968.

Anderson, Frederick R. NEPA in the Courts: A Legal Analysis of the National Environmental Policy Act. Baltimore: Johns Hopkins University Press, 1973.

Anderson, Walt (ed). Politics and Environment. California: Goodyear Publishing Co., 1970.

Baumol, William J. The Theory of Environmental Policy. Englewood Cliffs, New Jersey, 1975.

Bachrach, Peter and Baratz, Morton. Power and Poverty. New York: Oxford University Press, 1970.

Bauer, Raymond and Gergen, Kenneth. The Study of Policy Formulation. New York: Free Press, 1968.

Bentley, Arthur. The Process of Government. Chicago: University of Chicago Press, 1908.

Boguslaw, Robert. The New Utopians. Englewood Cliffs, New Jersey: Prentice-Hall, 1965.

Brenner, Michael. The Political Economy of America's Environmental Dilemma. Massachusetts: Lexington Books, 1973.

Bross, Irwin. Design for Decision. New York: MacMillan, 1953.

Burch, William (ed). Social Behavior, Natural Resources and the Environment. New York: Harper and Row, 1972.

185

Caldwell, Lynton. "Environmental Quality as an Administrative Problem," Annals of the American Academy of Political and Social Science, (November 1972), CCCXCIX-CCCC, pp. 103-115.

Caldwell, Lynton (ed). Environmental Studies: Paper on the Politics and Public Administration of Man-Environment Relationships, Institute of Public Administration. Bloomington, Indiana: Indiana University Press, 1967.

Caldwell, Lynton. A Challenge to Modern Society. New York: Doubleday, 1971.

_____. In Defense of Earth: International Protection of the Biosphere. Bloomington, Indiana: Indiana University Press, 1972.

Cobb, Roger W., and Elder, Charles D. Participants in American Politics: The Dynamics of Agenda Building. Boston: Allyn and Beacon, Inc., 1972.

Commoner, Barry."Alternate Approaches to Environmental Crisis," American Institute of Planners Journal, XXXIX, 1973.

Cooley, R.A. Congress and the Environment. Washington: University of Washington Press, 1970.

Crain, R.L. Politics of Community Conflict: The Flouridation Decision, Indianapolis: Bobbs-Merrill, 1969.

Crenson, Matthew. The Un-Politics of Air Pollution. Baltimore: Johns Hopkins University Press, 1971.

Council on Economic Priorities. The Price of Power: Electric Utilities and the Environment. Cambridge: M.I.T. Press, 1973.

Dahl, Robert. A Preface to Democratic Theory. Englewood Cliffs, New Jersey, 1965.

_____. Modern Political Analysis. Englewood Cliffs, New Jersey, 1965.

Daneke, Gregory and Lagassa, George. Energy Policy and Public Administration. Lexington, Massachusetts: Lexington Books, 1980.

Davies, Clarence. The Politics of Pollution. New York: Pegasus, 1970.

Dole, S.H., and Papetti, R.A. <u>Environmental Factors in the Production and the Use of Energy</u>. Rand Corporation, 1973.

Dorfman, Robert, and Dorfman, Nancy (eds). <u>Economics of the Environment</u>. New York: W.W. Norton, 1972.

Downing, Paul B. (ed). <u>Air Pollution and the Social Sciences</u>. New York: Praeger, 1971.

Dror, Yehezkel. <u>Public Policy Reexamined</u>. San Francisco: Chandler, 1968.

Ducsik, Dennis W. (ed). <u>Power, Pollution and Public Policy</u>. Cambridge: M.I.T. Press, 1970.

Dworsky, Leonard B. <u>Pollution</u>. New York: Chelsea House, 1971.

<u>Ecology and Politics in America's Environmental Crisis</u>. Policy Memorandum Number 37. Princeton: Center of International Studies, 1970.

Edel, Matthew. <u>Economics and the Environment</u>. Englewood Cliffs, New Jersey: Prentice-Hall, 1973.

Edelman, Murray. <u>The Symbolic Uses of Politics</u>. Urbana, Illinois: University of Illinois Press, 1964.

Energy, <u>Economic Growth and the Environment</u>, Washington, D.C.: Resources for the Future, 1971.

Enloe, Cynthia H. <u>The Politics of Pollution in a Comparative Perspective</u>. New York: David McKay, 1975.

Esposito, John. <u>Vanishing Air</u>. New York: Grossman, 1970.

Etzioni, Amitai. <u>The Active Society: A Theory of Societal and Political Processes</u>. New York: Free Press, 1968.

Ewald, William. <u>Environment and Change and Environment and Policy</u>. Bloomington, Indiana: Indiana University Press, 1968.

Fabricant, Neil and Hallman, Robert Marshall. <u>Toward a Rational Power Policy</u>. New York: G. Braziller, 1971.

187

Farris, Martin T., and Sampson, Roy J. Public Utilities: Regulation, Management, and Ownership. Boston: Houghton Mifflin, 1973.

Freedman, Ann Kolker, and Cohen, Jeffrey C. The Environmental Impact of Supplying Power to the Con Edison Service Territory: 1975-1980. New York: Citizens for Clean Air, August 1975.

Freeman, A., Haveman, Robert and Kneese, Allen. The Economics of Environmental Policy. New York: J. Wiley, 1973.

Friedman, David S., Electric Power and the Environment, Energy Policy Staff, Office of Science and Technology, G.P.O., August 1970.

Garney, Morris, and Hebbs, James (eds). Social Science and the Environment. Boulder: University of Colorado Press, 1967.

Garvey, Gerald. "Environmentalism Versus Energy Development: The Background to Environmental Administration." Public Administration No. 2, August 1975, pp. 328-332.

_____. Energy, Ecology, Economy. New York: W.W. Norton, 1972.

Goldman, Marshall I. Ecology and Economics: Controlling Pollution in the 1970's. Englewood Cliffs, New Jersey: Prentice-Hall, 1972.

Gordon, Kermit (ed). Agenda for the Nation. Washington, D.C.: Brookings Institute, 1968.

Gore, William J. and Dyson, J.W. The Making of Decisions. New York: Free Press, 1964.

Grad, Frank. Environmental Control: Priorities, Policies and Law. New York: Matthew Bender & Co., 1971.

Hage, Jerald and Riken, Michael. Social Change in Complex Organizations. New York: Random House, 1970.

Hagevik, George H. Decision-Making in Air Pollution Control. New York: Praeger, 1970.

Hardin, Garrett. "The Tragedy of the Commons," Science, CLXII, December 12, 1968, p. 1243-1248.

Harte, John and Socolow, Robert H. (eds). *Patient Earth.* New York: Holt Rinehart and Winston, 1971.

Haskell, Elizabeth H. and Price, Victoria S. *State-Environmental Management.* New York: Praeger, 1973.

Healy, Timothy. *Energy, Electric Power and Man.* San Francisco: Boyd and Frazer, 1974.

Heilbroner, Robert. *An Inquiry into the Human Prospect.* New York: Norton, 1974.

Helfrich, Harold (ed). *Agenda for Survival.* New Haven, Connecticut: Yale University Press, 1971.

Hellman, Richard. *Government Competition in the Electric Utility Industry.* New York: Praeger, 1972.

Hibbard, Benjamin Horace. *History of the Public Land Policies.* Madison, Wisconsin: University of Wisconsin, 1924.

House, William. "Rational Decision-Making Under Conditions of Risk," *Southern Journal of Business*, No. II, (January 1967), pp. 31-40.

Hurley, William D. *Environmental Legislation.* Springfield, Illinois: Charles C. Thomas, 1971.

Huxley, Aldous. *The Doors of Perception.* London: Chatto and Windus, 1960.

Jaffe, Louis L., and Tribe, Laurence H. *Environmental Protection.* Chicago: Bracton Press, 1971.

Jarret, Henry, (ed). *Perspectives on Conservation.* Baltimore, Maryland: John Hopkins University Press, 1958.

Jones, Charles O. *Clean Air: The Policies and Politics of Pollution Control.* Pittsburgh, Pennsylvania: University of Pittsburgh, 1975.

_____. "Speculative Augmentation in Federal Pollution Policy Making," *Journal of Politics*, XXXVI, No. 2, (May 1974), pp. 438-464.

_____. *An Introduction to the Study of Public Policy*. Belmont, California: Wadsworth Publishing, 1970.

Journal of Air Pollution Control. (Diverse Issues).

Kariel, Henry. *The Decline of American Pluralism*. Stanford, California: University of California Press, 1961.

Kaufman, Irving R. "Power for the People," *New York University Law Review*, XLVI, (November 1971), pp. 867-878.

Kohlmeir, Louis M. *The Regulators*. New York: Harper and Row, 1969.

Lahtey, John and Edmunds, Stahrl. *Environmental Administration*. New York: McGraw Hill, 1973.

Latham, Earl. *The Group Basis of Politics*. Ithaca, New York: Cornell Press, 1952.

Lawrence, Robert (ed). *New Dimensions to Energy Policy*. Lexington, Massachusetts: Lexington Books, 1979.

Levin, M. *Community Planning: Issues in Public Policy*. New York: Praeger, 1969.

Leventhal, Harold. "Environmental Decision-Making and the Role of the Courts." *University of Pennsylvania Law Review*, CXXII (January 1974), pp. 509-555.

Lindblom, Charles. *Intelligence of Democracy*. New York: Free Press, 1965.

_____. and Braybrooke, David. *A Strategy of Decision*. New York: Free Press, 1963.

Linton, Ron M. *Terracide*. New York: Paperback Library, 1970.

Lowi, Theodore. *The End of Liberalism*. New York: W.W. Norton, 1969.

Lundquist, Lennart. *Do Political Structures Matter in Environmental Politics*. Paper delivered at International Political Science Association, World Congress, Montreal, August 1973.

Luxenberg, Stan. "Who's Enforcing Air Pollution Law in New York?" *New England*, (April 1975), pp. 42-45.

McConnell, Grant. _Private Power and American Democracy_.
New York: Random House, 1966.

McClellan, Grant S. _Protecting Our Environment_. New York:
H.W. Wilson, 1970.

Mack, Ruth. _Planning on Uncertainty_. New York: J. Wiley, 1971.

Mann, Dean (ed). _Environmental Policy Formation_. Lexington,
Massachusetts: Lexington Books, 1981.

Mansfield, Harvey C. _A Short History of OPA_. Office of
Temporary Controls, (Washington, G.P.O.), 1947.

Meek, Ray L., and Straayer, John A. _The Politics of Neglect_.
New York: Houghton Mifflin, 1971.

Metcalf, Lee and Reinemer, Victor. _Overcharge_. New York:
McKay, 1967.

Milbraith, Lester and Inscho, Frederick R. _The Environmental
Problem as a Political Problem: An Agenda of Environmental Concerns for Political Scientists_. Paper delivered
at International Political Science Association World
Congress, Montreal, August 1973.

Miller, Edwin S. _Economic Analysis of Environmental Problems_.
New York: Columbia University Press, 1975.

Murdoch, William (ed). _Environment-Resources, Pollution
and Society_. Stamford, Connecticut: Sinauer Association,
1975.

Nagel, Stuart (ed). _Environmental Politics_. New York:
Praeger, 1974.

_____. _Incentives for Compliance with Environmental
Law_. Paper delivered at International Political Science
Association World Congress, Montreal, August 1973.

New York Association of the Bar, _Electricity and the
Environment_. St. Paul.,Minnesota: West Publishing
Co., 1972.

Newfield, Jack and DuBrul, Paul. _The Abuse of Power_.
New York: Viking Press, 1977.

Nicolson, Max. _The Big Change._ New York: McGraw Hill, 1973.

Niebuhr, Reinhold. <u>Moral Man and Immoral Society</u>.
   New York: Scribner and Sons, 1960.

Odum, Howard T. <u>Environment, Power and Society</u>. New York:
   J. Wiley, 1971.

Oelschlaeger, Max. <u>The Environmental Imperative: A
   Socio-Economic Perspective</u>. Washington, D.C.: University Press of America, 1977.

O'Hanlon, Thomas. "Con Ed: The Company You Love to Hate,"
   <u>Fortune</u>, 1966, V, pp. 122-127.

Ophuls, William. <u>Prologue to a Political Theory of the
   Steady State: Investigation of the Political and
   Philosophical Implications of the Environmental Crisis</u>.
   Dissertation, Yale University, 1973.

Oppenheimer, Jack and Miller, Leonard A. "Environmental
   Problems and Legislative Responses." <u>Annals of the
   American Academy of Political and Social Sciences</u>,
   CCCLXXXIX, (May 1970), pp. 78-86.

Ostrom, Vincent. "Human Fallibility, Political Theory
   and the Environment." <u>Policy Studies Journal</u>, (Summer
   1973), pp. 205-208.

Paulsen, David F. and Denhardt, Robert B. <u>Pollution and
   Public Policy</u>. New York: Dodd, Mead, 1973.

Perloff, Harvey S. <u>The Quality of the Urban Environment</u>.
   Washington, Resources for the Future, Inc., 1969.

Peterson, Phyllis. <u>Con Edison (B)</u>. Papers of Harvard
   Business School, 1974.

Petroleum Industry Research Foundation, Inc. <u>The East
   Coast Residual Fuel Oil Market - A Forecast to 1977</u>.
   June 1972.

<u>Pollution Control: Perspectives on the Government Role</u>.
   New York: The Tax Foundation, 1971.

<u>The Power Industry and the Public Interest</u>. New York:
   Twentieth Century Fund, 1974.

<u>Public Utilities Fortnightly</u>. (Diverse Issues).

Prisendorf, Anthony. "Con Ed: The Arrogance of Power,"
   <u>Nation</u> CCIV (March 27, 1967), pp. 401-404.

Regional Energy Consumption. A Joint Study by the Regional
    Plan Association, Resources for the Future, 1974.

Rehfuss, John. Public Administration as a Political Process.
    New York: Charles Scribner's & Sons, 1973.

Revelle, Roger and Landsberg, Hans. America's Changing
    Environment. Boston: Houghton Mifflin, 1970.

Rickles, Robert and New York Board of Trade (eds). Energy
    in the City Environment. New York: Noyes Press, 1973.

Ridgeway, James. The Politics of Ecology. New York: E.P.
    Dutton, 1970.

Ridker, R.G. Economic Costs of Air Pollution, Studies and
    Measurement. New York: Praeger, 1967.

Roberts, Marc. "Is there an Energy Crisis," Public Interest
    XXXI, (September 1973), pp. 17-37.

Roos, Leslie, Jr. Politics of Ecosuicide. New York: Holt,
    Rinehart and Winston, 1971.

_____. Studying Environmental Policy-Search for a
    Methodology. Paper prepared for International Political
    Science Association, World Congress, Montreal, Canada,
    1973.

Rosenbaum, Walter A. The Politics of Environmental Concern.
    New York: Praeger, 1973.

Ruedisili, Lon C. Perspectives on Energy and Environment;
    Issues, Ideals and Environmental Dilemmas. New Jersey:
    Oxford University Press, 1975.

Schacter, Esther Rodetti. Enforcing Air Pollution Controls.
    New York: Praeger, 1974.

Saltonstall, Richard and Page, James, Jr. Brown-Out and
    Slow-Down. New York: Walker & Co., 1972.

_____. Your Environment and What you Can Do About
    It: A Citizen's Guide. New York: Walker, 1970.

193

Sayre, Wallace and Kaufman, Murray. <u>Governing New York City</u>. New York: W.W. Norton, 1960.

Sax, John R. <u>Defending the Environment: A Strategy for Social Action</u>. New York: Knopf, 1971.

Schattschneider, E.E. <u>The Semi-Sovereign People</u>. New York: Holt, Rinehart and Winston, 1960.

Scott, David L. <u>Pollution in the Electric Power Industry</u>. Lexington, Massachusetts: Lexington Books, 1973.

_____. <u>The Economics of Environmental Pollution: The Case of the Electric Power Industry</u>. Lexington, Massachusetts: Lexington Books, 1973.

Seale, Robert L. and Sierka, Raymond A. (eds). <u>Energy Needs and the Environment</u>. Tuscon, Arizona: University of Arizona Press, 1973.

Shepherd, William and Gies, T.G. (eds). <u>Utility Regulation</u>. New York: Random House, 1966.

Simon, Herbert. <u>Models of Man</u>. New York: J. Wiley, 1957.

Stern, Arthur. <u>Air Pollution</u>. New York: Academic Press, 1968.

Talbot, Alan. <u>Power Along the Hudson: The Storm King Case and the Birth of Environmentalism</u>. New York: Dalton, 1972.

Thompson, Dennis L. (ed). <u>Politics, Policy and Natural Resources</u>. New York: Free Press, 1971.

Thompson, James. <u>Organization in Action</u>. New York: McGraw Hill, 1967.

Thompson, Victor. <u>Decision Theory, Pure and Applied</u>. New Jersey: General Learning Press, 1971.

_____. <u>Bureaucracy and Innovation</u>. Alabama: University of Alabama Press, 1971.

_____. <u>Modern Organization</u>. New York: Knopf, 1961.

<u>Transition Papers</u>. I, Fund for the City of New York, 1974.

194

Truman, David. The Governmental Process. New York: Knopf, 1951.

Utton, Albert, and Henning, Daniel H. (eds). Environmental Policy. New York: Praeger, 1973.

Vennard, Edwin. The Electric Power Business. New York: McGraw Hill, 1970.

_____. Government in the Power Business. New York: McGraw Hill, 1968.

Wade, Larry. Elements of Public Policy. Ohio: Charles E. Merrill, 1972.

Ways, Max. "How to Think About the Environment." Fortune LXXXI, No. 3, (February 1970), pp. 98-101.

Wandesford-Smith, Geoffrey. "The Bureaucratic Response to Environmental Politics." Natural Resources Journal XI, No. 3 (July 1971), pp. 479-488.

Welfrich, Harold.W. (ed). Environmental Crisis. New Haven, Connecticut: Yale University Press, 1970.

Wengert, Norman. Natural Resources and Political Struggle. New York: Random House, 1955.

Wilbrich, Mason. "Electric Facilities Siting." Virginia Law Review LVIII, (February 1972), pp. 257-334.

Wildavsky, Aaron. "Aesthetic Power or the Triumph of the Sensitive Minority over the Vulgar Mass: A Political Analysis of the New Economics," Daedalus 96, (Fall 1967), pp. 1115-1129.

_____. The Politics of the Budgetary Process. Boston, Massachusetts: Little, Brown & Co., 1964.

_____. "The Strategic Retreat on Objectives," Policy Analysis, II, No. 3, (Summer 1976), pp. 499-526.

Wolff, Robert Paul. The Poverty of Liberalism. Boston, Massachusetts: Beacon, 1968.

Wolozin, H. The Economics of Air Pollution. New York: W.W. Norton, 1966.

Worster, Donald (ed). American Environmentalism 1860-1915. New York: J. Wiley, 1973.

Young, Louise B. Power Over People. New Jersey: Oxford University Press, 1973.

Zeigler, Harmon. Interest Groups in American Society. Englewood Cliffs, New Jersey: Prentice-Hall, 1964.

Zurhorst, Charles. The Conservation Fraud. New York: Cowles Book Co., 1970.

REPORTS

Electric Power and the Environment, Energy Policy Staff, Office of Science and Technology, Washington, D.C.: General Printing Office, August 1970.

United States Presidential Science Advisory Committee, Restoring the Quality of Our Environment, White House, Washington, November 1965.

Bureau of Technical Resources, Department of Air Resources, No. 4, Major Point Sources, 1972.

_____. Data Report, Aerometic Network, 1970 thru 1974.

Con Edison Monthly Report on Generation and Transmission, Public Service Commission Case 25293, December 31, 1970.

_____. Environmental Report, Astoria #6, January 1972.

Comments on Pt. 410, Chapter IV, Title 42, Code of Federal Regulations by the New York Department of Environmental Conservation.

First Annual Report of the Mayor's Interdepartmental Committee on Public Utilities, City of New York, 1971.

Second Annual Report of the Mayor's Interdepartmental Committee on Public Utilities, City of New York, 1972.

First Annual Report of the Council on Environmental Quality, Washington, D.C., August 1970.

Ingram, Hollis, S. A Study of Thermal Pollution Abatement Methods, Division of Air Resources, New York State Department of Health, March 1, 1961.

_____. New York State Air Pollution Control Cost Study, Division of Air Resources, New York State Department of Health, February 1961.

Majority Report. Interdepartmental Committee on Public Utilities, New York, July 31, 1970.

Minority Report, Interdepartmental Committee on Public Utilities, New York, July 31, 1970.

New York City's Power Supply Development and Resources Corp., October 28, 1969.

2nd Session, House of Representatives, Reorganization Plan No. 3, No. 110364, December 1970.

GOVERNMENT DOCUMENTS

U.S. Congress, U.S. House Committee of Science and Astronautics, Subcommitttee on Science, Research and Development, Environmental Quality, 90th Congress, 2nd Session, January-March 1968.

U.S. Congress, U.S. Joint Committee on Atomic Energy, Environmental Effects of Producing Electric Power, 91st Congress, 1st Session, 1969.

U.S. Congress, U.S. House, Committee on Merchant Marine and Fisheries, Report to Accompany H. R. 12549, 91st Congress, 1969.

U.S. Congress, U.S. House, Committee on Interstate and Foreign Commerce, Subcommittee on Communications and Power, Hearings on Power Plant Siting and the Environment, 91st Congress, 1st and 2nd Sessions, 1969, 1970.

197

U.S. Congress, U.S. Senate, Committee on Commerce, Subcommittee on Energy, Natural Resources and Environment,
"Hearings on Report Covering the Principle Policy
Questions Now Facing the Environmental Protection Agency,
91st Congress, 2nd Session, 1970.

U.S. Congress, Joint Economic Committee, The Economy,
Energy and Environment, Environmental Policy Division
of the Legislative Reference Service, 91st Congress,
2nd Session, September 1, 1970.

U.S. Congress, How Can Our Physical Environment Best be
Controlled and Developed? Document No. 91-66, Legis-
lative Reference Service, Washington, D.C., 91st
Congress, 1970.

U.S. Congress, U.S. House, Committee on Interstate and
and Foreign Commerce, Bills Relating to Power Plant
Siting, 91st Congress, 1st Session, 1971.

U.S. Congress, U.S. Senate, Committee on Interior and
Insular Affairs, Reorderings in Economic Growth in
Relation to Population and Economic Growth, Prepared
by the Environmental Policy Division, 92nd Congress,
1971.

U.S. Congress, U.S. Senate, Committee on Interior and
Insular Affairs, Hearings on New Technology of the
Environment Acceptable to the Generation of Electricity,
92nd Congress, February 8, 1972.

U.S. Congress, U.S. Senate, Committee on Commerce, Subcommittee on the Environment, Energy and Environmental
Objectives, Document No. 93-68, Part 1, Washington, D.C.,
93rd Congress, 2nd Session.

U.S. Congress, U.S. Senate, Hearings before the Committee
on Interior and Insular Affairs, Financial Problems of
the Electric Utilities, 93rd Congress, August 7 and 8, 1974.

U.S. Federal Power Commission, National Power Survey Task
Force on the Environment, 1971.

GLOSSARY

AEC	Atomic Energy Commission
APCO	Air Pollution Control Office
CEPA	City Environmental Protection Agency
DAR	Department of Air Resources
DEC	Department of Environmental Conservation
EPA	Environmental Protection Agency
FEO	Federal Energy Office
FPC	Federal Power Commission
GNP	Gross National Product
HEW	Department of Health, Education and Welfare
ICPU	Interdepartmental Committee on Public Utilities
KW	Kilowatt hour
MSA	Municipal Services Administration
MW	Megawatt hour
NAPCA	National Air Pollution Control Administration
NEPA	National Environmental Policy Act
NEPCO	New England Petroleum Company
PASNY	Power Authority of the State of New York
PHS	Public Health Service
ppm	particles per million
PSC	Public Service Commission
SIP	State Implementation Plan
TVA	Tennessee Valley Authority
WQO	Water Quality Office (federal)

NOTE: Con Edison Arthur Kill #3 generating plant is the same
as Arthur Kill #30, and Ravenswood #3 and Ravenswood #30
refer to the same plants.

ABOUT THE AUTHOR

Regina Axelrod is the chairperson of the Department of
Political Studies and is on the faculty of the Institute
for Suburban Studies at Adelphi University. She has
specialized in environmental and energy policy and de-
centralization of urban government. She is the author
of Environment, Energy, Public Policy: Toward a Rational
Future (Lexington: Lexington Books, 1981) and has chaired
numerous professional conference panels on energy and
environmental policy. Currently, Dr. Axelrod is investi-
gating the environmental impact of massive coal-conversion
in the New York City metropolitan region. Dr. Axelrod
directed the Conference on Energy and Environment, June 8-9,
1979, at Adelphi University. She received the Ph.D. from
the Graduate School of the City University of New York
in 1978.